A BUSINESS OF YOUR OWN

A FUTURE YOU CAN COUNT ON
A Guide for Business Ownership
Acquiring a Going Business
Starting a New Business
Creating Lasting Value
Securing Your Future

THEODORE FOLKERT

outskirts
press

A Business of Your Own
A Future You Can Count On
All Rights Reserved.
Copyright © 2017 Theodore Folkert
v2.0

The opinions expressed in this manuscript are solely the opinions of the author and do not represent the opinions or thoughts of the publisher. The author has represented and warranted full ownership and/or legal right to publish all the materials in this book.

This book may not be reproduced, transmitted, or stored in whole or in part by any means, including graphic, electronic, or mechanical without the express written consent of the publisher except in the case of brief quotations embodied in critical articles and reviews.

Outskirts Press, Inc.
http://www.outskirtspress.com

Paperback ISBN: 978-1-4787-7645-1
Hardback ISBN: 978-1-4787-8263-6

Cover Photo © 2017 thinkstockphotos.com. All rights reserved - used with permission.

Outskirts Press and the "OP" logo are trademarks belonging to Outskirts Press, Inc.

PRINTED IN THE UNITED STATES OF AMERICA

Table of Contents

Introduction i
Chapter 1 - The Basics of Entrepreneurship 1
Chapter 2 - Understanding Business Operations 9
Chapter 3 - The Process of Self Employment 17
Chapter 4 - Selecting the Type of Business 23
Chapter 5 - Buying an Existing Business 38
Chapter 6 - A Business Plan for Buying a Business 49
Chapter 7 - Starting a New Business 63
Chapter 8 - A Business Plan for Starting a Business 67
Chapter 9 - Financing Alternatives 80
Chapter 10 - Introduction to Franchises 87
Chapter 11 - Franchise History 91
Chapter 12 - Franchise Opportunities 101
Chapter 13 - Franchise Ratings 103
Chapter 14 - Evaluating Franchise Opportunities 110
Chapter 15 - Growing and Expanding Your Business 114
Chapter 16 - Private Equity Groups 122
Chapter 17 - Operating Financial Models 130
Conclusion 144
Glossary of Financial Terms Used in this Publication 151
Index 155

Introduction

WOULD YOU LIKE to be your own boss and have more control over your future income and success? Would you like to run a business the way you think best, make your own decisions, hire who you like, serve who you like, set your own hours, reap the rewards from your efforts? Would you like to build value in the business that you can redeem personally at some point, either in a future sale of the enterprise or through absentee management in retirement? Or maybe you could work there the rest of your life at whatever level you desire or pass it on to a family member?

Owning and managing your own business can be challenging but it can also be quite rewarding. It can be an alluring and gratifying alternative to a lifetime as an employee for a big or small company, a job where you may have little incentive and limited opportunity to achieve stature or income commensurate with your efforts and contributions.

Employment has become more and more challenging in the last few decades. This has left many of us with less assurance of earning a sustainable income without the anxiety of possible devastating interruptions. The employment picture in this country has changed significantly since I joined the work force about fifty years ago. Many of those who preceded me by a generation or two or who joined the work force in my generation looked at employment somewhat differently than do the majority of employees today.

Some of you may recall a Dilbert cartoon by cartoonist Scott Adams. The boss man states that *"the company is going to start monitoring employee productivity in real time. Any questions?"* Dilbert says *"I need one clarification. Are you saying you removed the last shred of human dignity from our jobs and reduced us to nothing but a meat machine that suffers in a state of perpetual inadequacy as each person is compared to an arbitrary and ever-growing goal until there is no realistic way for the employee to find happiness through natural means?"*

The boss man says, *"That's one way of looking at it."* This is of course meant for humor, but it makes a point and emphasizes a challenge that some of us are confronted with in the employment process.

A few decades ago most company owners and managers considered employees an asset of the company, along with the other assets – the product lines, trade secrets, inventory, fixtures, equipment, and customers. Many companies considered workers or employees as career members of the organization and provided opportunities for advancement and the feeling of protection, stability of income and benefits for a lifetime of employment. The new term of reference today for those companies who still value employees as assets is "human capital" or "human resources." Although this is a rather impersonal classification for human beings, as opposed to "employee" or "co-worker," it is meant to represent employees as being of considerable value to the success of the company.

For many employers today, employees are often considered expendable at a moment's notice, with little consideration of the employee's past contributions to the company or his or her ability to find and qualify for other employment opportunities. Human capital is more often only a considered value when specialized skills are required and then on a more limited basis. A few decades ago lifetime careers were more readily available in most any industry, especially in manufacturing, which provided employment for a much larger percentage of the work force than today. Now, in many industries, manufacturing employees are not even considered human capital.

The availability of the global labor market, foreign competition, and the ease of off-shoring production to low wage markets, has provided an attractive option for employers in most manufacturing industries and has consequently made the formerly valued employee expendable – no longer considered human capital.

There are many reasons to explain the difference in the employment situation and most of the reasons center on the employers. Having been a business owner and an employer for more than forty years, I have watched the changes take place. Some of the factors that have made employment less secure can be explained by consolidation of industries; some by the growth of behemoth retail establishments; some by technology; some by the focus of the corporations on short-term results as opposed to longer term results – short-term share value instead of long-term growth. One of the most likely culprits is the global economy and the competition of lower wage countries in performing manufacturing, distribution, sales, and clerical functions at a price that the employer not only cannot resist but actually pursues for survival. Where the cost of labor and materials controls the cost of goods and services and the market competition controls the selling price, you either meet or beat the competition or you are out of the game.

No matter how we explain the changing employment environment, the fact is that a lifetime career with one company, the opportunity to climb the ladder of success, with wage increases, vacations, health care, promotions, and retirement benefits, is becoming less likely. Corporation owners are focused on short-term profits, and like sport team owners, have a policy of demanding immediate and short-term results from their managers. This means that the manager, if he or she wants to continue to manage, must make the numbers in order to stay in the game. Failure to produce to the level established by the owners of the company means that the individual will more than likely be out the door and replaced by another career-seeking and upwardly mobile individual. The same policy trickles down to employees through the manager. If employees want to stay in the game they must make the numbers. The loyalty and attitude of we're all-in-this-together is often no longer a guiding principle for management. Now the attitude has often changed to expendable-at-a-moment's-notice. In the last few years, we have seen empirical evidence of the devastating effect of loss of position on many of those holding middle management positions. Thousands of middle-aged middle managers who lost their positions had disappointing results in their job-seeking efforts. Many spent years on unemployment benefits which were insufficient to maintain their lifestyle. To this day many still fail to find employment adequate to sustain their family's livelihood.

Another major effect on the changing employment environment is the rapidly changing technology. Many of the jobs previously performed by individuals are now being performed by machines. This started many decades ago with farming technology and has ramped up in the last fifty years with thousands of manufacturing functions. When I was in the machining and manufacturing business in the 1980s we had automated machinery that could machine parts faster and more accurately than any person could. Since those days this technology has multiplied and spread over most all of the manufacturing industries. Some machines can be programmed to run all day and all night, with minimal supervision, and produce high quality products – often higher and of more consistent quality than could be produced by the employee.

We see the results of employee elimination everywhere we go. Many checkers are being eliminated at the grocery markets by automatic checker machines and many bank tellers have been replaced with automatic teller machines. Now there is an ATM on practically every corner. Many parking garage cashiers have been replaced by automatic collection devices. Many clerical jobs have been replaced by the advance of word processing and computer technology. Where stenographers and dictation machines took the information and a clerical person typed it, more often than not, the person dictating simply does the typing and printing. More and more shopping is being done online, reducing the demand for store clerks and often even retail space.

As manufacturing has continuously been off-shored to lower wage countries some manufacturing centers around the country have become blighted industrial sites and some cities and states have become heavily burdened with debts and expenses but less tax income. Some blame the free-trade agreements, the North Atlantic Free Trade Agreement and the Central American Free Trade Agreement - perhaps rightly so. Some of it is due to tired and antiquated facilities and some to obsolescence, but much is attributable to technological advancements and developing countries with lower wages.

The leading economists and scholars don't seem to give us much hope for the employment situation to change significantly in the near future. Most of our high school graduates and even many of our college graduates are having difficulty finding career opportunities or good paying jobs that can support a family. Many are remaining with their parents due to the inability to find adequate employment to support living alone or starting a family life of their own while retiring massive student loan debt.

No matter the reasons to which the economists attribute the decline, the fact remains that the employment situation has changed and there doesn't seem to be much we can do about it in a short time. Those who have special education, training or abilities are in a better position than some, but there is no assurance that the security of any technology, job, or function will continue unabated. Although the thought of joblessness is stressful for all of us, we have to look at all possibilities to find our niche in the economy and to assure ourselves of a viable income. Such consideration and search for your niche, your sustainable livelihood, may take you in the direction of self-employment or owning your own business.

The following chapters of this book provide a discussion of the advantages and disadvantages of being your own boss and the requirements, responsibilities and processes of selecting your path to success by founding a business, assuming control of an existing business, or simply becoming a specialist in some field and developing a customer base for yourself as a sole practitioner. You will gain a much better understanding of the direction to take in securing your role in the business world. The discussion of the basic functions of self-employment and business management will give you the essential steps necessary to make a prudent decision regarding your chosen self-employment niche.

If this endeavor seems like a solution to your future livelihood and success, you should find this book enlightening and helpful in moving forward with knowledge of the essential steps to success and the cautions against failure.

CHAPTER 1

The Basics of Entrepreneurship

ENTREPRENEURSHIP, THE ACT of organizing and managing a business enterprise, has been a path to success for many of us - giving us the opportunity to follow our dream, to launch an enterprise, to grow it to a viable size, and to create value from our own efforts. The attraction of entrepreneurship has always been enticing for those of us who have been less than satisfied with the option of working for others and more inclined to do our own thing, to be our own boss.

As an entrepreneur in various companies for many years and simultaneously as a business advisor and business broker, I have come to realize the impact of these changing conditions of employment as they encourage the entrepreneurial spirit. Many times over the last twenty years I've counseled with employees who'd become disenchanted with their employment and employment opportunities. Many thought they had careers but came to realize that the career notion was empty anticipation and had become elusive at best, encouraging them to seek opportunities that would give them more control over their future and free them from being subject to capricious employers focused on personal success and unable or unwilling to recognize or appreciate the human capital value of their employees.

The difficult job market and the uncertainty of its improvement have made the prospects of entrepreneurship of much greater interest. The value of controlling one's own destiny and escaping the uncertainty of the employment market has encouraged many of those who were or could have been employees to seek business ownership or self-employment enterprises. The perceived lack of viable opportunities in employment have come to outweigh the inherent risks of entrepreneurship and the fear of failure for many aspiring career seekers.

Entrepreneurship can be the answer for many, but it isn't for everyone. If you have a strong desire to have more control over your future, the willingness to accept the challenge, the perseverance to stay with it, self-confidence and a tolerance for risk and stress, you may be well suited for the challenge of business ownership. These are not essential prerequisites or mandatory requirements; but they are certainly useful traits in the formation, promotion and operation of your own business.

With the evolving technology and reordering of the relationships between employers and employees, particularly the disappearance of career or lifetime employment opportunities, small business ownership may be the most promising path to prosperity for many skilled or unskilled workers, including you. It can give you more control over your future and an opportunity to be rewarded for your efforts directly rather than as only one member of a huge organization. It can erase the fear of losing your job due to circumstances beyond your control. These include business failure or acquisition by another company, obsolescence of a product or service, downsizing, lack of competitiveness, the actions of inconsiderate or misinformed superiors, or personality conflicts.

There are a number of ways to approach business ownership. You can start from scratch with some knowledge of a certain type of business, you can assume management and then ownership of a company over time, or you can acquire an established company and assume a going concern with some record of success and some promise of a rewarding future.

There are pros and cons for each way of approaching business ownership. A start-up is generally somewhat risky. A good many start-ups fail within a few years - but they can be very successful if based on an organized planning effort, good knowledge of, and experience in the industry, adequate initial capitalization, and sources of additional capital if and when needed.

Buying an established business can be risky if done haphazardly. It is a good approach to entrepreneurship if all of the possibilities and pitfalls are fully considered in advance and a prudent and comprehensive examination is completed, and like a start-up, if the planning, knowledge, and capital are sufficient to enhance the likelihood of success.

Establishing oneself as a sole practitioner can result in an intolerably cyclical income and an unreliable level of support for your standard of living, but if planned like a business and promoted and managed properly can provide a rewarding future with satisfying control of your own destiny.

Statistics about Small Business

Big businesses didn't start out that way; they all started out small. It would be interesting to know how many businesses started in someone's garage or basement. Hewlett Packard was founded in 1939 by Stanford University classmates, Bill Hewlett and Dave Packard, in a small garage in Palo Alto, California. They started out designing and fabricating electronic devices, selling them to the Disney Company and others.

Another company we are all aware of also started tiny. Apple, founded by Steve Jobs and Steve Wozniak, began in 1976 when they built and began marketing their first computer. Look at where Apple is today.

How about Microsoft, Facebook, Google, Twitter, and now, Snapchat, and other technological and social media companies? I assume some of these started either in someone's garage or in similar facilities. I believe Snapchat started at home. I leased them their first office at Venice Beach, which they outgrew very rapidly and have now expanded into much larger quarters in order to accommodate a company with many employees and a market value estimated in the billions of dollars.

The pioneers who started these companies, although they had high hopes, didn't know how successful they would be. They all started out small and undercapitalized with no assurance of success. They had the desire to benefit from their own efforts, confidence in their ideas, and the stamina to withstand the fear of failure.

The Small Business Administration (SBA) tells us there are approximately 23 million small businesses in this country. Of course, they have a different view than most of what is small. They consider any business with less than 500 employees to be a small business. Most of us would consider many of these big businesses.

The SBA tells us that small businesses provide more than 50% of the jobs in this country. They tell us that small businesses occupy more than 30% of all commercial space, more than 20 billion square feet. They tell us that, since 1990, big businesses eliminated 4 million jobs and small businesses added 8 million new jobs.

We can compare figures provided by the United States Census Bureau, which tells us that, of their count of 27 million firms, about 6 million of them have one or more employees and represent an annual payroll of more than $5 trillion. They tell us that there are less than 20 thousand big businesses, with more than 500 employees, representing an annual payroll of about $3 trillion. The remainder of the 6 million are small businesses, with fewer than 500 employees, and represent an annual payroll of about $2 trillion.

The American Small Manufacturers Coalition tells us that manufacturing in the U.S. represents about 12 percent of our gross domestic product (GDP), that figure the economists are always referring to, which represents the total value of goods and services produced. The Department of Commerce tells us that 98 percent of the manufacturers are classified as small businesses and that small and midsize businesses do about 33% of our exportation to other countries. Small firms are able to be more flexible and can be more adaptable to a customer's needs and therefore can be on the leading edge of innovation and development. There are many government programs which give small firms an opportunity to grow through contracting with the government for the supply of thousands of products each year.

Knowing these figures, which were all derived from public sources, is not crucial except for the fact that they emphasize the value of small businesses and demonstrate that many of them are very successful, creating value for those who start them and build them into sustainable enterprises as employers of about 50% of the 120 million employees in the country.

Just think about who you engage every day for goods and services that you need. The coffee shop, the restaurant, the market, the car wash, the auto repair service, the plumber, the lawn service, the cleaners, the retail stores, the internet technology expert – the list could go on – but you can see that most of these services we engage daily are provided by small business owners – i.e., entrepreneurs, who started small with a good business plan and survived as successful business owners.

So, it can be done and you can do it if you have a viable plan and follow the steps necessary to make it work.

Duties of Entrepreneurs

Typical small business owners wear lots of hats and have the ultimate responsibility for the various functions of the business. These include: administration, production, marketing, sales, finance, employment matters, and completion of customer requests and orders. Every aspect of the business is the owner's personal responsibility. Every function must be understood. Pointing the finger at an employee for some failure or uncompleted function is no longer a solution. You, the owner, are responsible and you, the owner, will gain or lose depending upon the performance of all functions of the business. This is a responsibility that you must be willing to accept and be capable of performing if you are to be a successful entrepreneur.

Obviously, we can't all be masters of all trades or all functions of operating a business. The more knowledgeable you become about all of the various functions of the business, the better you can perform them. You can also understand the type of employee to select to perform them, and recognize shortcomings or inadequate performance. Most successful business owners would probably agree that they prefer to do the functions of the business themselves that they do best, or that require their personal attention, and to assign the remainder to other employees, professionals, or vendors who specialize in those functions.

Once a business establishes itself and grows to a sufficient size, it is common to separate management functions into various roles, such as: president or chief executive officer (CEO) who oversees the company in its entirety, a chief operating officer (COO) who oversees operations, a chief financial officer (CFO) who oversees all financial functions of the company, a human resources director to oversee employee administration, a sales manager to oversee all sales and customer relation functions, a production manager to schedule and manage production, or an office manager to oversee all office functions. For a small business, most of these functions are performed by the owner initially. As the company grows, the duties and responsibilities become more intense. Some require specialization and the full-time attention of a dedicated manager.

Of course, all businesses will not have the need to engage all of these specialized functions. It depends on the size of the company and importance of each function to the success of the company. If your company continues to operate successfully as a small enterprise you may continue to provide most of these functions yourself and keep a tight grip on all of the critical aspects of the business. One thing entrepreneurs should remember in the development of the management structure is that, although the specialized ability of various managers can make for a more professionally run company, control of the decision-making process by the owner of the business is diminished somewhat with each level of management, as functions are assigned to others and performed separately. So, management structure requires much consideration in order for it to enhance effective growth and to control damage by incompetent or ineffective managers.

Business Organizations

There are various types of organizational structures to utilize. A business can be organized as a sole proprietorship, a general partnership, a limited partnership, a limited liability company, a corporation, a subchapter S corporation or a public company. These organizational structures have differing legal liability features and taxation features. Selecting the right structure for your business should be done along with the advice of your accountant and attorney, who have specific knowledge of the taxation and liability issues which should be considered.

The various business organizational structures are as follows:

- **Sole Proprietorship** – the company is generally owned and operated by one person who is responsible for the operation and receives all of the profits of the company. The IRS reports that there are more businesses organized as sole proprietorships than any other. The sole proprietor can be held personally responsible for all of the company's debts and liabilities. The company can be operated under a fictitious name which usually must be registered as such with the county where the company is located.
- **General Partnership** – the company is owned by two or more partners who are all responsible for the operation. Each partner receives the partner's share of profits and is responsible jointly and severally for all debts and liabilities of the partnership. Profits are taxed as personal income for the partners.
- **Limited Partnership** – there must be one general partner that acts as the controlling partner and has unlimited liability for the debts and liabilities of the partnership. Other partners are usually limited to liability for the amount of the participation in the partnership.

- **Limited Liability Company** – the company is owned by two or more members and can be formed as a corporation or as a partnership and is taxed and has protection from liabilities similar to a corporation
- **Corporation** – the company is formed as a legal entity separate from the owners and is owned by shareholders who are not responsible for the liabilities of the company. Profits of the company are subject to taxation as a corporation and when distributed to the shareholders are taxable to the shareholder. Corporations are formed under a state charter and must submit articles of incorporation and by-Laws for the charter for approval by the Secretary of State of the given state. There are generally requirements of annual corporate minutes and annual registration of the corporation with the state.
- **Subchapter S Corporation** – a corporation which elects to pass profits through to the shareholders, like a partnership, which are then taxed on an individual basis. The incorporation requirements are the same as a C corporation. The election to be taxed as an S corporation is for taxation purposes.
- **Public Company** – a corporation owned by many shareholders with shares registered and available for purchase or sale under rules of the Securities and Exchange Commission (SEC). There are stringent rules and regulations required by the SEC and annual reports that must be submitted. The costs of financial reporting required by the SEC usually limit the use of the public company structure to larger companies that can absorb the cost and arduousness of the process.

Most small businesses start out as sole proprietorships. Many of them become corporations as they begin to grow due to the preference of the limited liability of the corporation owners. The individual shareholders are not responsible for the debts or other liabilities of the corporation.

CHAPTER **2**

Understanding Business Operations

IN ORDER TO discuss and understand the operation of a business and the necessity of a viable size and profitability, we will examine the format of a profit and loss statement for a small business.

For those who may not be familiar with financial terms, we will review some simple ones:

- **Assets -** what the company owns. This would include furniture, fixtures, equipment, inventory, patents, copyrights, real estate, leasehold improvements, and other investments.
- **Liabilities** – what the company owes. This would include accounts payable for material and supplies, equipment loans, real estate loans, working capital loans, equipment leases, and company purchase financing.
- **Revenue** – what the company takes in for a specific period. This would include all sales of products and services and the sale or use of company assets.
- **Cost of Sales** – the costs of products or services. This includes material, labor and outside services that are direct costs of producing or providing services.
- **Profit Margin or Gross Profit** – the income remaining after deducting direct costs.

- **Operating Expenses** – what the company pays out for a specific period other than direct costs deducted under cost of sales. This would include all operating expenses, including: rent, wages and salaries, insurance, auto expenses, utilities, supplies, professional fees, and any other expenses incurred in operating the business.
- **Profit or Earnings** – what the company earns for a specific period after all direct costs and operating expenses are deducted.

A simple profit and loss statement might look something like the illustration below. The statement on the left would be the most current month and the statement on the right would be the six month period just ended:

ABC Company Profit / (Loss) Statement June, 2013			ABC Company Profit / (Loss) Statement June 30, 2013 Year-to-Date	
Total Sales		30,000	Total Sales	200,000
Cost of Sales		18,000	Cost of Sales	120,000
Gross Profit		12,000	Gross Profit	80,000
Expenses			Expenses	
Advertising		500	Advertising	3,000
Auto		1,000	Auto	4,000
Insurance		500	Insurance	4,000
Legal & Accounting		200	Legal & Accounting	1,200
Office Expense		1,000	Office Expense	6,000
Payroll		3,000	Payroll	18,000
Rent		2,000	Rent	12,000
Taxes, Licenses		200	Taxes, Licenses	1,000
Telephone		100	Telephone	600
Utilities		500	Utilities	3,000
Other		1,500	Other	6,000
Total Expenses		**10,500**	**Total Expenses**	**58,800**
Profit/(Loss)		**1,500**	**Profit/(Loss)**	**21,200**

UNDERSTANDING BUSINESS OPERATIONS

If we analyze these income and expense categories we can get an understanding of the way the business functions:

Sales - sometimes referred to as revenue, this includes the total of sales or services sold for the period. For an ongoing business this number has some history but for startup projections it must be estimated. The estimate can be based upon some evidence of presold services, accounts that seem committed to engage the services of the company or sales of similar businesses in the area or industry. The danger for a startup is over-estimating this number and the period of time it may take to achieve the estimated level of business. A startup projection should allow for the period of time required to build a business to a projected level and provide for capital to cover any shortfall in the interim.

Cost of Sales - Cost of sales, sometimes referred to as cost of goods sold, is the cost of material, services, and sometimes labor to produce or provide the product or service. It could be the cost of the merchandise for a retail store, the cost of food and the preparation staff for a restaurant or the cost of labor, material and outside services for manufactured products. The rules are not cast in stone as to what is included in this category but the value of it is to realize the total cost of production or inventory and to calculate the profit margin to cover administrative, sales expenses and profit of the company.

Gross Profit (Profit Margin) - The gross profit (or profit margin) is the total sales minus the cost of sales. This number is important because the financial success of the business depends upon the profit margin being adequate to cover the operating and administrative expenses and yield a profit for the owners of the business. If the profit margin is too thin, it is difficult for the business to survive. If it is too strong, it may make it difficult to compete with others in the same area or industry. This determination must be made based upon industry and area information which will vary for different industries and different locales.

Expenses - All expenses other than those included in cost of sales must be included as operating expenses. These will include all of the expenses listed in our sample above as well as any others. The statement above illustrates a simple cash flow of the business. To provide a complete income statement, other items would be included, such as: amortization and depreciation, which are non-cash deductions of asset purchases spread over a period of years, as required by tax laws.

Profit / (Loss) - The profit or loss from the business for the period indicated is then calculated and provides the business owner with the basis to determine if the volume of business, the pricing of goods and services and the control of operating expenses is adequate to sustain the business or if the volume, prices or expenses need to be adjusted in order to be successful.

Analysis of the Profit / (Loss) Statement - By examining the above statement we can draw some conclusions about the income or projected income. It appears that the salaries do not include any income for the owner or manager of the business. If the sale price for the goods and services can be adjusted upwards, that could help the equation, but the competition in the industry may not allow such a pricing adjustment. If the costs of sales and operating expenses cannot be adjusted to provide more profit then the business must generate additional sales, and a higher gross profit, in order to make the business sustainable. If the owner requires an income from the business of $60,000 annually, then average monthly sales of $40,000 would be required, otherwise the business venture may not be feasible.

A word of caution for prospective business owners - it is easy to over-estimate results when attempting to justify an investment of time and money in a business venture, so caution is recommended. The better you can justify and support your estimates and projections the more realistic are projections that might otherwise be overly optimistic.

The figures used in the above illustration are not meant to be accurate or recommended sales, expenses or profits, but merely an example of the use of the financial statement to determine results of a company or feasibility of an anticipated enterprise.

Insurance - It is of utmost importance for the business owner to be properly insured for loss of company assets and for protection for claims of liability for damage or injury to others. Losses from casualties and liability can inundate a company of any size, particularly a small company.

Types of insurance that some companies may require for proper risk management:

- **Casualty insurance** - for buildings, leasehold improvements, machinery, equipment, fixtures, vehicles and inventory – a loss of any or all of these assets can be devastating for a company. They should be insured to the replacement value. If an uninsured casualty should occur it could bankrupt the company.
- **Liability insurance** – a company should be insured for liability for loss due to damage or injury to persons or property of others. This could be due to injury on the business property or away from the property if an employee or company product is held responsible.
- **Product liability insurance** – a company should be insured for liability for loss due to damage or injury to persons or property of others caused by a product or service provided by the company.
- **Worker's compensation insurance** – a company should be and, in most states are required to be, insured for liability for loss due to damage or injury to employees in the process of performing their duties for the company.
- **Life insurance** – in some cases a company may be required by a lender, or may elect to carry insurance on the owner of the company, certain managers, or other key employees who are critical to the continued success of the company.

Payroll records and taxes - All employers are required to keep records of employee earnings and to deduct and pay over to the proper taxing authorities the payroll taxes and deductions for Social Security, Medicare and other taxes, such as unemployment insurance funds and job training funds of various states.

Reports and tax deposits are required to be filed with the state on a monthly or quarterly basis. Payroll tax liabilities can be a source of difficulty for many small companies if diligence is not exercised in making timely reports and deposits. Penalties and interest for delinquencies can increase the liabilities significantly. Business owners usually cannot avoid the responsibility for collecting and paying over to the state and federal government the correct amounts, even in the event of the business ceasing to exist. The owner or other responsible party can be held liable for such deductions and payments, so it is of utmost importance for this requirement to be executed properly.

In most cases small companies are much better off engaging a payroll service such as ADP, which is probably one of the oldest and largest companies providing such service, or any similar payroll company to perform the payroll service. In such service the payroll company receives the payroll information from the employer, calculates the payroll, payroll taxes, and deductions for all of the employees, deducts the total to be deposited with the state and federal government by debiting the employer's bank account, and prints the payroll checks on the employer's bank checks.

The payroll company keeps all of the records and makes all deposits in a timely manner, sends the employer copies of all reports, and stays current on all changes in deductions with all of the taxing agencies.

Utilizing payroll services can be advantageous for the business owner in terms of timeliness, accuracy, and by not diverting management's attention from more vital functions in operating and growing the business.

Caution is recommended in selecting a payroll service. Payroll service companies generally collect the taxes due from the employer and pay them to the taxing authorities. If they default in their fiduciary responsibilities, the employer remains responsible for the taxes due, regardless of the contract between the employer and the payroll company. Any dispute or claim of misrepresentation or fraud would be of no concern to the taxing authority.

UNDERSTANDING BUSINESS OPERATIONS

Laws, rules and regulations - Federal, state, and local laws often require various permits, licenses, and clearances in order to lawfully operate a business. These are enacted and required for assurance of qualification to perform certain services or distribute certain types of products. They may be required for the protection of consumers or businesses from fraud or misrepresentation. They may be required for compliance with environmental laws or regulations.

Such licenses or permits may require certain types of liability or casualty insurance, surety bonds, performance bonds, health permits, police permits, tax clearances, background checks, or certifications of specific knowledge of the industry. A license or permit may require specific study courses and examinations indicating sufficient knowledge of the industry. In some instances a permit may require advanced education with credentials verifying completion of required schooling in the industry.

Prior to launching a new business enterprise one should contact the governmental agencies applicable with any given type of business. This may entail contacting a federal government agency, the Secretary of State, or the City Clerk to assure compliance with any required permits or licenses for the industry or region in question.

Business Facilities - Prior to launching a new enterprise one should investigate and possibly select adequate facilities for the start-up that will be sufficient for the initial few years of operation. This could include office space, shop space, warehouse space, or parking spaces.

The type of space, the requirements, and the importance of specifics will vary for different types of business. For example: a restaurant or other business may require good visibility, easy access, sufficient pedestrian or vehicular traffic, and sufficient local businesses or residences. The selection would be more critical than an office, manufacturing facility, or warehouse that would not be visited by the public.

For businesses dependent upon visibility and heavy traffic, a poor location can cause failure from the beginning, so the selection is one of the most important factors in the process.

There are many factors which should be included in any location selection process. These would include: the rental cost of the space, the initial term of the lease, renewal terms, periodic or renewal increases in rent, maintenance, building services, utilities, insurance requirements, termination terms for the landlord or the tenant, and any other terms of a rental agreement that may affect the operational or financial aspects of the business. For those who are unfamiliar with leasing terms and negotiations it is advisable to engage a real estate agent specializing in leasing to assist throughout the process. There should be certainty that the zoning for the location allows the type of business being launched. This can be determined by contacting the county or city agency that establishes and enforces zoning restrictions.

Accounting, Legal and Banking - A business owner without a background in finance or law should engage an accountant and an attorney to review financial and legal matters that could affect the business.

An attorney who is in the regular practice of business law and is familiar with the advantages of organizational types and local and state requirements should prepare organizational documents and counsel the owner regarding all legal matters and governmental requirements which would apply to the business.

A certified public accountant, (CPA) should be engaged to set up the financial books for the company and advise the owner on organizational types and taxation matters which could affect the new enterprise. The accountant could prepare regular financial statements and provide financial counsel for the owner to assist in maintaining a financially healthy operation, with adequate working capital for an efficient operation and maintenance of good relationships with customers and vendors.

A local bank should be selected to handle the banking needs of the company. The bank should have a staff which works regularly with small enterprises and that is familiar with lending requirements that could benefit the new enterprise initially and on an ongoing basis.

CHAPTER 3

The Process of Self Employment

THE DECISION TO become self-employed could be one of the most important decisions you will ever make about your future. You can't just stick your toe in the water to test it. You have to dive in. You need to make sure you can swim even if the water gets a little rough. Therefore it deserves some serious planning and soul searching. There are many questions you need to ask yourself regarding your path to self-employment.

First of all, what are the objectives you wish to achieve in becoming self-employed? Do you plan to be a sole practitioner of some profession or special skill? Do you plan to start a business requiring facilities and employees? Do you have a specific industry or type of business in mind? Do you have a special education or skill? Do you have experience in a profession, job or industry in which you wish to engage? Do you plan for a permanent situation or an interim livelihood until a better opportunity comes along?

What is your level of funding? Do you have access to funds to acquire a business? Do you need to earn a living immediately upon launching your career or business or can you sustain your livelihood for a period of start-up time while you are establishing a reliable cash flow?

A word of caution for prospective entrepreneurs - one important fact that you should think about is that no one is ever totally self-employed. No matter what you do or how you do it there is someone you must answer to. That someone is your customer to whom you provide services or products. You have probably heard the old Bob Dylan song, *Gonna Have to Serve Somebody* - "…. *It may be the devil or it may be the Lord, but you're gonna have to serve somebody.*" That is so true when it comes to managing a business; you have to serve somebody. The better you serve them, the better are your chances for continuing to serve them. The old saying that the customer is always right isn't really true. The customer isn't always right, but the customer is always the customer, and must be served.

There are many ways of being self-employed. You could provide handyman services, maid services, car repair services, electronic repair services. You can teach music or foreign languages. You could be a nanny for working mothers. You could be a real estate salesperson or broker. You could be an internet technician or cable TV installer. You could be a taxi or limousine owner/driver. You could be an attorney, accountant or some type of counselor. You could do consulting work in some field in which you have expertise. Whatever way you choose to be self-employed must be well thought out and the upside and the downside should be fully defined and considered.

Another word of caution – it is important to realize that upon becoming a business owner the record keeping is all on you from now on. Whatever your business entity is, you are responsible for your own income taxes, Social Security and Medicare payments as provided by law. None of the customers you serve will be responsible for such reporting as your former employer did when you were employed. If this important function is overlooked or ignored, it can be costly.

Sole practitioners

You can be your own boss as a sole practitioner, specializing in a service that many companies wouldn't typically have a full time employee to perform. There are many functions or careers in which the individuals could be identified as sole practitioners. Below are a few services provided by those who prefer being self-employed as sole practitioners.

THE PROCESS OF SELF EMPLOYMENT

- Accounting – some accountants develop a private practice by serving a few clients with bookkeeping and tax reporting services. The sole practitioner sometimes fulfills a client's desire for more personal attention regarding such matters and perhaps more attractive pricing of such services.
- Acting – actors would typically be sole practitioners since they are hired for a specific role in a play, TV show, or movie and are paid individually for each role performed.
- Attorney representation – many attorneys have individual offices or shared offices with others and are sole practitioners. Some clients prefer the special attention, better access, and negotiable pricing of a private attorney, as opposed to that provided by some larger firms.
- Auto repair – some auto mechanics operate individually from a small shop with no employees, serving local businesses, neighborhood customers, family, and friends. By controlling the overhead costs that larger facilities with more employees incur, service can be priced more competitively.
- Bookkeeping – some entrepreneurs who have accounting experience with small businesses operate as sole practitioners. This provides the personal service and sometimes significant savings for these services that small firms enjoy and enables the small firms to have more accurate accounting and reporting than would be accomplished in house with less knowledgeable employees.
- Construction service – many construction services are performed by individuals who specialize in certain crafts, such as: painting, roofing, concrete finishing, carpentry, electrical, plumbing, and others, serving customers they receive through word-of-mouth, reputation, or local advertising.
- Consulting – there are many types of consultants who operate as sole practitioners in fields such as: real estate, business sales, marketing, advertising, lending, business management, finance, risk management, engineering, architecture, and many others.

- <u>Counseling</u> – some counselors prefer to operate as sole practitioners in such fields as: marriage counseling, behavioral counseling, anger management, and education.
- <u>Entertainment</u> – many in the entertainment field are sole practitioners, such as: musicians, actors, comedians, public speakers, show hosts, party planners, wardrobe specialists, set designers, stage hands, film and sound technicians, and disc jockeys for private events.
- <u>Internet technology</u> – computerization and internet technology have created roles for many sole practitioners for computer installation and repair, networking, internet advertising, software code writing, website design and development, email campaigns, and search engine optimization.
- <u>Journalism</u> – some journalists are successful sole practitioners, writing and syndicating their articles or selling them individually to media publishers. Most novelists and business writers operate individually and publish their materials once written through publishing companies and major book retailers.
- <u>Landscaping</u> – landscaping needs for businesses and homes has made it possible for many individuals to develop a base of regular customers and generate a steady stream of income as sole practitioners.
- <u>Language instructing</u> – there are many language instructors who develop a private business teaching foreign languages. Business is generated through advertising or word-of-mouth.
- <u>Personal services</u> – many beauticians, hair stylists, barbers, manicurists, masseurs, masseuses, seamstresses, housekeepers, landscapers, and others prefer to operate as sole practitioners.
- <u>Tutoring</u> – many parents choose to engage tutors to help their children with their learning, sometimes for special needs, sometimes for preparation for college entry exams.
- <u>Taxi Service</u> – although taxi service historically has not been a sole practitioner business, it has become more so with the

advent of Uber and other online taxi solicitation services which operate with individual owner-operators of vehicles who respond to requests for taxi service and establish their own charges for service, locale, and hours of service.

As sole practitioners of these professions and trades, each individual is responsible for developing his or her customer base, providing the service, collecting payment, accounting for their income and expenses, paying their payroll taxes to governmental agencies, insuring their operations, and continuing to solicit new customers to balance any attrition of the level of business they require.

A sole practitioner's monthly profit and loss statement might look something like the below illustration:

Joe Jones Carpentry Profit / (Loss) Statement June, 2015	
Customer Receipts:	
Customer #1	3,500
Customer #2	2,300
Customer #3	3,200
Total Receipts	**9,000**
Material Costs	(3,400)
Gross Profit	**5,600**
Expenses:	
Advertising	50
Auto	250
Insurance	200
Legal & Accounting	50
Office Expense	50
Taxes, Licenses	150
Telephone	50
Other	200
Total Expenses	**1,000**
Profit/(Loss)	**4,600**

A BUSINESS OF YOUR OWN

The figures used in the above illustration are not meant to be accurate or recommended sales, expenses or profits, but merely an example of the use of the financial statement to determine results of a company or feasibility of an anticipated enterprise.

The number of businesses in the U.S. classified as non-employee firms by the U.S. Census Bureau is more than 20 million. It is assumed that most of these are sole proprietorships operated entirely by one individual. So, it is easy to assume that the success of sole practitioners is widespread and that there are far more firms operating as such than with any other classification.

If you have any special skill, experience, or education, you can become a sole practitioner. You can start and operate from your home with one client and build it from there as you develop a reputation. Many small businesses and large businesses started out home-based and, as they grew, expanded into rented facilities, hired employees, and added customers, growing into a viable size and becoming an asset for the owner who started as one.

CHAPTER 4

Selecting the Type of Business

SELECTING THE TYPE of business to buy or launch should be of primary importance to enhance your chance of success. You should match your personal abilities and financial capabilities with the industry or field of business in choosing those opportunities you wish to pursue.

Some important considerations in the selection process:

- Are there any requirements of personal knowledge or professional credentials for the business you are considering?
- What financial resources are required to start and continue operations?
- What is the demand for the product or service and what is the trend of growth or decline?
- What are the chances of competing in the industry or the area?
- Will employees with specialized skills be required and, if so, what is their availability?
- What will be the financial requirements for expansion?
- Consider your education. Are you educated or trained for any certain profession or trade? Have you had any special education in business practices, accounting, marketing, legal issues, or other?

- What kind of background do you have in various types of businesses? In what industries have you been employed--what products or services?
- What is your investment capability? Do you have personal savings, funds from others available for your use, or pre-approved credit facilities?
- In what geographic area do you prefer to operate your business?
- Do you plan to operate a home-based business or a place of business where you can accommodate customers or employees to assist you?
- What type of business do you think you would enjoy being involved in for many years to come?
- What will be the start-up time required in order to reach a profitable level?
- What level of income will be required for you to be satisfied with the success of your business?

Business types to consider

This section provides some features of certain types of businesses in order to provide an understanding of the requirements and potential pitfalls which could affect a business venture. These thoughts can be applied to any type of business while weighing the financial demand, employee capability requirements, marketing challenges, and the risk of failure. You should make your own determination by considering the issues, features, and requirements of various types of business, and evaluating the requirements and risks.

Auto Rental - Establishing an independently owned and operated auto rental agency can require a large investment. For a franchise with an established company, the investment would be much less, requiring funds for facilities, furniture, fixtures, rental of parking space for rental cars, and working capital. Typically the franchisor would provide the vehicles, which would be the largest cost for a privately unfranchised operation. The most important considerations would be

SELECTING THE TYPE OF BUSINESS

location, location, location. There must be a demand in the area you choose and you must be able to compete with the other companies in the area. The risk of failure would be lack of demand for rentals and operating costs that are uncontrollable as growth occurs, with the primary consideration being adequate space to accommodate a growing inventory of available vehicles. In the budgeting process, as a private, unfranchised owner, one should give careful thought to vehicle maintenance and adequate insurance for vehicle damage and liability.

Auto Repair – An auto repair facility can be established in many different ways. A one-bay garage can suffice initially but would not be recommended. Auto repair requires analysis of the problem, contracting for the service required, ordering and waiting for parts, completion of the repair, and acceptance of payment upon delivery. Consequently, a repair facility should have more than one bay, auto lifting equipment if required, paint booth facilities if required, outside parking area for cars awaiting repair, and some type of office for administrative duties, such as dealing with customers, accepting payment, and accounting functions. The risk of failure would be lack of demand in the area, poorly trained repair persons, poor workmanship, over- or underpricing of services to compete, and limited facilities for expansion.

Auto Sales – Auto sales facilities can require substantial investment, not only initially, but ongoing. Most auto dealers start out with used cars. As a used car dealer, one should have numerous vehicles to offer potential customers. A used car dealer would typically not have initial financing and would need to have available funding for a good inventory. One should have a thorough knowledge of vehicle types, conditions, market values, and costs of preparation for resale. Trade-ins are often part of the deal when selling a car, so the dealer must have knowledge of appraising vehicles of all types. There are sources available to provide current estimated values for all types of vehicles, but the dealer must consider the condition of the trade-in and the cost of preparing it for resale or selling it to a wholesaler or other dealer. The risk of failure would be improper appraisal of vehicles, lack of effective sales and advertising programs, and economic cycles affecting potential buyers. As used car dealers prove to be successful over a period of time, financing can be obtained from local bankers. This enables expansion. However, if the economy flounders, the dealer must service the floor plan of bank financing regardless. This factor has bankrupted many car dealers during hard times.

Bar, Cocktail Lounge – The required investment for bars and cocktail lounges can vary considerably depending upon the location, size, and profitability. They can provide a living income for one individual or a return on investment for investors. They can be a safe investment and easy to resell. All of this depends upon the type of facility, the length of the facility's lease, and the typical clientele. Most bars serve some type of food, so they are also engaged in food service, which increases the responsibility and personnel required. The risks of failure include pilferage of inventory by employees, unauthorized complimentary drinks for favorite customers, embezzlement of cash sales, penalties for serving minors, loss of the lease, loss of alcohol license, or unaffordable rent increases. Bars are typically easy to resell to a new owner. However most of them operate in leased facilities requiring landlord approval of assignment of the lease to a third party. This can have an adverse effect on the price or the sale of the business. The lease is one of the most important aspects of ownership. Loss of lease or unaffordable rental terms can cause failure. Moving to another location would be very costly. The biggest investment would be leasehold improvements. If you have to move, you generally are required to provide the leasehold improvements for the new location.

Computer Related – There are many business opportunities in computerization: wholesale sales, retail sales, installation, internet technology, networking, equipment repair, programming, website creation, search engine optimization, data storage, data recovery, website hosting, and others. Any of these businesses requires special training, knowledge, and experience. Any of the areas of computer technology can become a business for those who have the expertise to provide the service required. Retail or wholesale distribution would require significant capital for inventory and would be subject to possible obsolescence of equipment due to the continuous upgrading of technology. Providing services such as installation, networking, and repair can be launched with one or more customers and built up with word of mouth or promotion. Expansion, however, would be restricted by the inability to obtain qualified technicians and not staying abreast of changing technology. Providing services such as programming, website creation, data storage, and website hosting would require special expertise in those functions and would likely require capital for development of capacity and staffing while generating sufficient clientele to provide a sustainable flow of business. The risks of failure of computer related businesses would include loss of customer base, inability to remain technologically proficient, lack of qualified personnel, technicians leaving employment and engaging the firm's clients, and failure to continually engage new clients.

Construction – There are many trades in the construction industry – excavation, carpentry, masonry, roofing, metal fabrication, plumbing, electrical, painting, flooring, heating and air-conditioning, and others. Some construction businesses specialize in one trade or another. Some are considered general contractors. Construction obviously requires special knowledge of the type of construction provided, both for the business owner and the employees who do the work. The required investment varies depending upon the machinery and equipment required and the amount of working capital required to finance work in progress until a job is completed and payment is received. Some small contractors who have established reputations are able to obtain an advance deposit to cover the investment in time and materials, as well as progress payments during construction. This provides some funding relief for the small contractor. Inability to have access to sufficient working capital can cause a construction company to fail due to the inability to start and complete jobs in a timely manner. The risks of failure are considerable. They include losses from under-bidding of contracts, defective workmanship, delayed contracts, financial failure of the customer, adverse economic conditions, and excessive competition.

Convenience Store – Convenience stores in good locations are typically successful for the small entrepreneur. Location, location, location are the critical features of successful convenience stores. A franchise such as 7 Eleven, Quik-Trip, or others in a well-chosen spot would enhance the chance of success. Many convenience stores now include auto fueling and thus would require substantial capital for launching a new facility. The cost of building construction, underground fuel tank installation, and the permitting process would require a large investment. With the planning, location approval, and name brand inclusion of a popular franchise, the chance of success is generally more assured than would be the case for an independent start-up. Many convenience store operators enter the business by acquiring a going establishment which is leased from a property owner. In this event the facilities would be established and the initial costs would include the acquisition of furniture, fixtures, equipment, inventory, as well as a consideration for goodwill based upon the income derived by the selling party. The risks of failure would include poor location, poor access, inefficient facility, limited merchandise, revenue control, and inadequate personnel.

Food Service – Food service is a popular but demanding business. There are many details requiring constant monitoring in food operations. Staffing is critical, along with inventory control, quality control, and punctuality of service. All are critical in order to maintain customer satisfaction. Food service requires an owner and employees with special knowledge of food preparation. Those in the industry are subject to the inspection and approval of the various health departments and must maintain specific standards in the storage and handling of foods, as well as compliance with stringent requirements regarding cleanliness and sanitation. Most first time entrepreneurs who wish to enter the food service business should give much consideration to a franchised restaurant opportunity. There are hundreds of choices available in all ranges of investment capability. By taking advantage of the proven success of food service operations available as franchises, one would increase the chances of success and limit the risk of failure. The risks of failure include: lack of sufficient business, inadequate staffing, dissatisfied customers, health department requirements, lease termination, unaffordable rental terms, and adverse economic conditions. Successful food service operations are often sought after by people looking for a successful business. Again, certain factors can be a deterrent on resale, such as: unaffordable rental terms, lack of lease assignment, health department violations, declining area, and inadequate income to support pricing for resale.

Freight Service – Freight companies often start out small with one vehicle and one customer. Growing larger in the freight business requires additional capital for equipment. There are many owner/operators in the trucking business whereby an individual owns the truck and hauls loads of freight on a contract basis. Owning a trucking company with numerous vehicles requires much more capital than acquiring a loan on one truck. A trucking company must have good bank financing in order to purchase and maintain the equipment required and to maintain the working capital to cover day-to-day operations in servicing freight contracts. The risks of failure include: lack of funding, lack of qualified drivers, lack of recurring freight contracts, and adverse economic conditions.

Hair Salons, Nail Salons, Barber Shops – Personal care services are generally businesses that can be started and operated with limited capital requirements. The exception would be leasehold improvements if the premises are not improved for the use desired. A single owner usually operates this type of business, utilizing one chair or station personally, and renting additional stations to others for a weekly fee or a percentage of the weekly sales. The risk of failure is not great unless the facility occupies space in a high rent area, which would require the owner to maintain a good staff of practitioners to support the high rent factor. In these establishments the loss of lease is not necessarily fatal since the owner can often lease space nearby and retain the customer base. The clientele for such businesses would be more inclined to stay with the owner than seek an unknown practitioner to replace them.

Health Clubs – Athletic facilities for staying in good physical condition are popular new business choices for first time entrepreneurs. Some provide aerobics classes, yoga classes, boxing training, martial arts training, body-building coaching, and other workout choices. These facilities can be profitable for a one person business on a small scale. The limiting factor is the number of members one can serve on an individual basis. Good promotion and staffing of additional practitioners in work-out training and massage services can enhance the income stream. Adding workout equipment to the offerings would require substantial capital due to the cost of equipment of latest technology, maintenance of equipment, and replacement of damaged or obsolete equipment. As additional functions of a health club are added, more space is required, which provides an additional overhead cost for facilities. The risks of failure would include lack of retention of member base, new competition in the immediate area, lack of qualified personnel, loss of facility lease, increase of facility cost, and lack of promotion of new members, which typically would be an ongoing requirement.

Insurance Services – Insurance agencies or brokerages typically do not require substantial capital to establish or operate. An agent or broker generally represents the insurance company, writes the insurance application for the client, and submits the application to the insurance company for approval. The insurance company, upon acceptance, receives payment of the premium and pays the agent or broker a commission on the premium. Some agents or brokers work from home. Those who build a sizable book of business generally establish an office conveniently located for the client base, staffs the office as needed, and employs other agents to acquire new business on a commission basis. The risk of failure would be negligible unless the insurance company or companies become dissatisfied with the performance of the broker. In the event of the insurance company changing the broker relationship, the broker could typically take their clientele to another company to maintain the insurance required by the client. The insurance agent generally establishes the personal relationship with the insured and engages the insurance company to provide the coverage.

Manufacturing – There are many different types of manufacturing businesses. Many of them would require substantial capital for machinery and equipment, inventory, and working capital. Manufacturing typically requires special knowledge on the part of the owner and many of the employees. Manufacturing is generally a long term business due to the facility requirements and the need to establish customers and contracts to sustain a continuous flow of business. Manufacturers with a proprietary product must have an established customer base for their product in order to maintain an adequate staff of qualified employees to provide the service required. They often must have a substantial line of credit in order to operate efficiently. The risks of failure include: inadequate personnel, declining customer base, declining product distribution, offshore competition, product obsolescence, and adverse economic conditions.

Printing – The printing industry has been adversely affected by the digital world. Much of the work that printers used to do can now be done by a desktop computer and printer. However, many printers have maintained their customer bases and level of business by providing those services that they can do better, and with more favorable pricing, than can be done in-house. Printing requires an investment in equipment and facilities and has become more capital intensive over the years as more sophisticated equipment has become available. Printing companies still provide much better quality work and can produce thousands of copies much more economically than a typical office. The risk of failure for printers would include: decline of customer base, forced relocation of the business, or competitors with more advanced processes that can outperform their equipment or provide better quality.

Real Estate Sales – Real estate sales organizations come in all sizes. Many are individuals operating from home or a small office. Some of those who have been around for a long time have become huge organizations, particularly with a consolidation of the industry that has transpired over the last few decades. A real estate salesperson can become an agent or a broker. In most states one must become an agent for a period of time before qualifying to become a broker. All real estate agents and brokers must be licensed by the state in which they operate. Licensing requires knowledge of the laws affecting property ownership and ownership transfer. An agent must be engaged by a broker to sell real estate. The broker typically maintains an office and employs numerous agents, who work on a split-commission basis. The risk of failure is not great in this industry unless the broker fails to control the overhead of the office. If the broker quits or sells the brokerage to another, the agent can stay on with the new broker or change to another broker, so the risk on the part of the agent is primarily in failing to produce sales. After a required period of time as an agent, the agent can obtain a broker license by applying and meeting the additional requirements imposed by the state.

Retail Sales – Retail stores can require substantial investment in leasehold improvements, furnishings, and inventory. A retail store owner would lease a store space, acquire merchandise, provide leasehold improvements, hire and train staff, and proceed to attract customers. The importance of the product line cannot be overstated. Uncertainty of the success of the product line can lead to a financial difficulty. It is difficult to change the product line in an efficient manner if it is not successful. The inventory investment, which consumes a large part of working capital, cannot be recouped quickly. The owner's overhead continues unabated all the while. Retailers with years of experience have a much better chance of success than a start-up retailer since they would typically have better judgment regarding product acceptance in a given area. Retail sales businesses have produced numerous business failures due to the cost of attractive retail space in popular retail facilities and the uncertainty of product acceptance by the customer base. That provides the greatest risk of failure for the new retailer.

Taxi, Limousine Service – Now that Uber, Lyft, and others of like kind have come about, the taxi business has changed. You can put your car into service with one of these online companies and be in business virtually overnight. Not so easy for the taxi companies. A taxi company is required to be approved by the police commission in many areas. The owner often must obtain a police permit. They are required to maintain special livery licenses, have their vehicles inspected regularly for safety and meter certification by the Department of Weights & Measures. The taxi drivers are also required to be licensed by the city within which they operate and qualify for a police permit. A taxi company generally must have numerous vehicles in order to provide efficient service due to the costs of providing efficient service. The company must maintain a 24 hour radio dispatch system. For a taxi company to be successful there must be enough business to accommodate several dozen vehicles. Otherwise, there would be insufficient income to cover the cost of advertising, liability insurance, dispatch staff, and vehicle maintenance. The risk of failure demands careful consideration for taxi companies, particularly due to the basically unregulated online ride-sharing industry which has grown enormously over the last few years.

The factors discussed above can serve as the basis for evaluating other types of business ventures in terms of start-up costs, working capital requirements, and inherent risks – risks which are prevalent in any type of business venture.

A BUSINESS OF YOUR OWN

The table below provides some characteristics of the investment level, special knowledge, and risk of failure of various businesses.

Business Type	Characteristics – Investment – Skills – Risk of Failure
Auto rental	Investment: facilities for renting, servicing and storing the rental vehicles. Location is important, risk of failure is minimal.
Auto repair	Investment: facilities for repair shop, tools, and equipment to accommodate services provided. Risk is minimal.
Auto sales	Investment: vehicle inventory and sales and storage facilities required. Knowledge of vehicle styles and values is of utmost importance. Risk of depreciation of unsold vehicles.
Bar/cocktail lounge	Licensing requirements. Investment: purchase of existing business or establishing a new location. Leasehold improvements can be prohibitive. Risk of failure is a concern.
Building cleaning	Must establish reliable contracts. Limited investment or skills required. Limited risk.
Carpentry	Special skills required. Instability of business flow can be problematic. Maintaining qualified workers a must.
Computer programming	Special skills required. Competitive in the general services area, special knowledge and latest technology a must.
Computer repair	Special skills required. Limited investment in facilities. Hiring technicians can be risky.

SELECTING THE TYPE OF BUSINESS

Construction	Special skills required. Instability of business flow can be problematic. High quality workmanship a must.
Delivery service	Limited investment required. Must establish enduring contracts. Drivers readily available. Limited risk.
Food service	Investment: Cost of buying an existing business or establishing a new location. Some special knowledge required. Risky for newcomers. Location important.
Freight service	Investment in equipment and facilities can be substantial. Some enter the business with one vehicle and contract with a larger company.
Hair salon	Investment: Acquiring an existing business or establishing a new location. Retention of technicians and customers a must. Location important in hiring and retaining practitioners.
Hotel or motel facilities	Investment: Substantial in acquiring an existing facility or establishing a new location. Association with a big name operator is essential for good occupancy.
Insurance sales	Typically no investment required unless acquiring an existing agency. Limited risk. Income may build slowly.
Lawn service	Limited investment on a small scale. Limited risk. Good area essential to establish a loyal base of business.
Limousine service	Investment can be substantial. Some start out with one vehicle and contract with a larger operator.
Manufacturing	Initial investment usually substantial. Good contracts essential to maintain

35

	steady flow of business. Special skills may be required. Can be risky.
Nail salon	Similar to hair salon. Limited investment unless acquiring an existing facility. Some investment in facilities. Location important in retaining operators.
Painting	Similar to construction. Demand for repainting of commercial and residential properties is common and can be competitive. Reliable workers essential. Limited risk.
Physical fitness training	Establishing a complete facility requires substantial investment for improvements and good equipment. Individual trainers can operate without facilities if a reliable customer base can be established.
Plumbing	Limited investment for vehicles and tools. Special skills required. Demand is usually reliable. Good, reliable technicians are essential.
Printing	Investment in facilities and equipment in acquiring an existing facility or establishing a new location. Must offer services that are not typically done in-house. Risky.
Real estate development	Special knowledge of property values, zoning requirements, and construction required. Substantial funding required for acquiring property, improving for desired use, and marketing to a buyer.
Real estate sales	Investment generally not required. Special licensing and knowledge of real estate values mandatory. Newcomers usually affiliate with large

SELECTING THE TYPE OF BUSINESS

	firms to learn the business and get established in the industry.
Retail sales	Investment required either for an acquisition of an existing facility or establishment of a new location. Investment in inventory. Location is critical. Can be risky.
Taxi service	Investment in equipment can be substantial. Some newcomers start with one vehicle and affiliate with a larger service company on a lease basis. Licensing is typically required. New online services are now available which can ease entry into the business.

The above indications of investment level, special knowledge, and risk of failure reflect the opinion of the author based upon experience in business ownership, business consulting, and business brokerage. The indications cited are variable depending upon the type and size of business, the level of the industry in which the party is involved, and the effort put forth by the business owner. Capital requirements will vary considerably depending upon facility requirements, machinery and equipment, inventory, accounts receivable, and other factors specific to various industries. The considerations discussed can be adapted to evaluate other business enterprises not mentioned.

CHAPTER 5

Buying an Existing Business

BUYING AN EXISTING business is often a good way to become your own boss. A carefully selected business that has existed for a period of years has generally passed the test of time, assembled a reasonably good management structure and staff, established a reliable customer base, abandoned unsuccessful strategies, and become a viable establishment in the market area and industry.

The important thing to focus on is the term "carefully selected." Without careful study and diligent selection, you could be buying someone else's problems. The company you acquire could be poorly managed and declining in acceptance by the company's customer base. It could be in a declining industry which is wrought with obsolescence. It could be undercapitalized in an industry undergoing technological advancements which require additional investment in product design, tooling, equipment or facilities. It could require expertise to continue, which the company lacks. All of these considerations should be fully investigated in an exhaustive study during the decision-making process. Your decision could be rewarding or it could be disappointing. You must have a strong belief that you can succeed. You may not soon get another chance if you fail and your investment of time and money is lost.

The process of buying a business deserves some serious thought and deliberation and should include some essential steps to help to assure a successful acquisition.

A business broker who specializes in representation of business buyers can be very helpful in your search for and analysis of business opportunities. Those with ample experience have sources of business opportunities, a good knowledge of business valuations, and have a good understanding of the offering, negotiation, documentation, and closing of business sale transactions.

The important steps to acquiring a company should include:

1. **Identify your objectives**

    If you would like to buy a business, what are your objectives? Obviously you wish to replace and improve your employment income, in which case you will probably be interested in buying a business with a reliable stream of income. Are you interested in acquiring a company with a reliable level of business or with significant growth potential? Do you have a specific industry or type of business in mind? Do you prefer a business in a specific geographic area? What are your areas of expertise, training, education or experience? Do you have business management experience that would be advantageous in a specific industry?

2. **Analyze the cost of fulfilling your objectives**

    How much income is necessary to fulfill your needs? How much money do you have available to acquire a business? Will it be from savings or borrowed money? If it is borrowed, what will be the repayment terms? If necessary, do you have sufficient income or savings to buy a business and sustain your living expenses for a period of time? Have you prepared a specific budget of your living expenses? Any shortfall of income required to cover your living expenses must be covered by the business you acquire or launch or it must be covered by savings or other sources.

3. Narrow your search

Unless you narrow your search to situations which will work for you, too much time and effort will be wasted and you may become discouraged before you find the right solution. Focus on the types of businesses that you would want to manage. Focus on geographic areas where you would be willing to operate. If you have no investors committed to join you, you should focus on acquisitions that you can manage financially. If you plan to attract other investors, you should focus on businesses large enough or with enough growth potential to make your proposals attractive to potential investors. There must be good profit potential and good growth potential; otherwise the offering may be too small to support you, the primary owner and manager, and provide a return on the investment for the investors.

4. Review the operations

Review the brief advertising profiles on potential acquisitions. Request additional information on those businesses in which you have significant interest. Continue to narrow your selection process. Focus on those businesses with the most obvious likelihood of sustainability of income and growth potential. As your level of interest continues, drive by the businesses of interest and get a feel for the area and the appearance of quality of the operations.

5. Review the historical and current financials of the business

Ask for profit and loss statements, income statements, and balance sheets from the previous few years and the current year-to-date. Study them thoroughly along with your accountant or advisor. Determine the actual cash flow of the operations. Consider previous growth of revenues and profits and the potential for future growth. Determine the initial capital required, as well as capital requirements for expansion, and for maintaining state-of-the-art facilities for current or new technology. Consider any potential decline in revenue which could occur if the current owner walks away, such as a declining customer base or the loss of key employees. Consider the viability of the industry and the area in which the business is operating.

6. **Determine the acquisition value**

In order to determine the acquisition value of the business for your purposes you should review the operating financial statements of the business you choose to pursue, along with the assistance of a financial advisor qualified to provide a business valuation.

The cash flow of the business, as a minimum, should be sufficient to repay the down payment over time, service any purchase financing, and provide adequate income for the owner. Businesses are valued based on variable criteria depending upon the objectives of the buyer. Most businesses of which the valuation is based strictly upon earnings, would generally be valued at a multiple of one to five times the supportable future annual cash flow, with smaller businesses typically falling into the lower end of the scale of multiples. Most business brokers generally state that small businesses sell for an average of one and one-half to two and one-half times the supportable cash flow. Some businesses sell for higher multiples of earnings and some for less. Some larger businesses are valued by buyers at greater multiples based upon strategies and synergies of the buyer, such as: market share, economies of scale, additional product lines or services, geographical expansion, territorial rights, and other intangible considerations. Bigger businesses are also generally more stable financially, with less risk of failure. Smaller businesses are generally considered more fragile, with a higher risk of failure.

A valuation of the business might result in an illustration such as this:

Acquisition Valuation Scenario	
Proposed Acquisition Price	$250,000
Other Acquisition Costs	15,000
Working Capital Required	75,000
Total Funding Required	340,000
Cash Investment – 40%	140,000
Financing Required 10 years @7.5%	200,000
Total Cash Investment	**$140,000**
Gross Sales of the Company	$750,000
Projected Cash Flow	150,000
Acquisition Financing Debt Service	(28,000)
Annual Improvements Anticipated	(10,000)
Expected Return on Cash Invested -10%	(14,000)
Discretionary Cash Flow	**$98,000**

The above illustration is not meant to suggest optimal business acquisition criteria, but an example of using financial information to determine if the acquisition makes sense for the buyer. Some call this a "Sanity Test."

In the above example the acquisition price would be determined by your evaluation of the business with the assistance of your financial advisors. The other acquisition costs would include fees for financial or legal advice, rent deposits, licenses required, or other initial expenses. The working capital represents the cash needed on hand to cover payroll and other operating expenses until customer payments are sufficient to provide timely payments. The projected cash flow would be determined through your review of historical financial information of the business. Debt service terms would vary depending upon the repayment terms negotiated with lenders. Annual improvements would be based upon any anticipated addition or replacement of furniture, fixtures, or equipment, or additional inventory required.

After fully considering all of the financial aspects of the acquisition, it is often advisable to obtain a third-party appraisal from a qualified firm specializing on business sale transactions.

An important aspect of evaluating a potential acquisition would be to identify the value drivers, such as:

- Longevity in business
- Industry trends
- Desirability of the business type
- Knowledge and training of workforce
- Proprietary products or services
- Patents or copyrights
- Trademarks or tradenames
- Diversification of products or services
- Exclusivity of products or services
- Exclusivity of distribution
- Exclusivity of supplier
- Unique processes
- Location favorability
- Reliable and diverse customer base
- Reputation in the industry
- Barriers to entry for new start-ups
- Healthy industry for growth
- Technological competence
- Certifications or licenses
- Favorable facilities leases
- Availability of growth capital
- Sustainable healthy profit margins
- Limited risk of failure

7. Interview the business owner

Meet with the business owner and tour the facilities. Ask about the history of the company – how it started, how it grew, the company's position in the industry or area, the employees, the customers, the facilities, and the future requirements. Ask about the owner's relationship with the employees and the customers, with the thought in mind of any potential loss of business or loss of key employees after a change of ownership. And above all, determine why the business is for sale. Is the owner retiring or entering into another business venture? Is he or she desiring the sell due to health reasons, family reasons, or other interests? Or is the owner leaving for some adverse reason of which you should become aware, such as: market decline, undercapitalization, or new competition that may adversely affect the revenue and profitability?

8. Study the industry and the area

You should do some research of the industry of your acquisition to determine the potential for growth or the presence of conditions which could lead to a declining market for the product or service. Consider the possible impact of new technology or obsolescence which could affect the industry. Determine if the business is capable of competing if new technology requires additional expertise or investment. Consider if the facilities, equipment, personnel and expertise are sufficient to compete now and in the future.

9. Verify your funding

Calculate your personal funding available for investment in the business and funding that may be necessary from other sources, such as bank financing, seller financing, or investors.

10. Consider the downside risks

What are the risks of failure of the business you have selected? Will any of the customers cease to do business with a new owner? Will any key employees leave the company for other opportunities? Will the industry decline due to economic reasons or cyclicality of the industry? Will the technology become obsolete? Will a qualified staff be replaceable in the area and at a cost that is feasible?

11. Prepare an offer

An offer usually consists of a letter of intent or purchase agreement, either of which would include the purchase price, the terms of payment, the assets and liabilities included, and all of the other terms of sale, such as: a period of due diligence for the buyer to carefully study the business, a period for approval of any financing required for the purchase price, a period of time for the seller's correction of any items required by the buyer in the offer to purchase, a specific date of the closing of the sale and possession by the buyer, a period of time for the seller to provide training and transition assistance, and terms of cancellation of the agreement by buyer for unacceptable and uncorrectable discoveries during due diligence or seller's failure to meet terms required in the agreement.

An offer can be presented verbally. However, in most all cases it should be presented in writing with as many of the above terms included as possible. Otherwise, an agreed purchase price can change significantly as terms not included in an accepted offer are negotiated after the fact.

An offer should be prepared by a financial advisor or an attorney familiar with business transactions so that all of the legal aspects are considered.

12. Negotiate a purchase and sale agreement

The offer to purchase or letter of intent, with any approved changes, can then become the final purchase and sale agreement or a final agreement can then be prepared by buyer and seller specifying all of the terms of the accepted offer or letter of intent. This agreement then can be submitted to the closing attorney or escrow agent along with any deposit required of buyer.

The agreement should include a negotiated tax structure based on tax strategy opinions from qualified sources, such as your CPA or attorney. Tax structure can have an important financial effect on the buyer or the seller. The seller may be faced with a stock sale scenario triggering double taxation of gain on the sale. The buyer may be faced with lack of or adverse depreciation schedules on assets acquired. These considerations can be important in determining the best type of sale structure for both parties. The seller may prefer an all-cash asset sale or an all-cash stock sale. The seller may prefer a down payment, along with seller financing. The allocation of assets, which is determined between buyer and seller, can affect tax strategies for the buyer or seller depending upon time sale terms versus all-cash for the seller or depreciation of assets for the buyer.

13. Due diligence

Due diligence should include a comprehensive study of the business by the buyer. All of the following aspects of the business should be considered:

- **Financial aspects** – sales, expenses, profits, growth trends, sustainability of sales and profits
- **Employee aspects** – adequacy, capability, future availability, pay levels, potential retention, key employees. If there are key employees who could leave and cause a costly interruption in the business, it should be avoided or dealt with in the valuation
- **Customer aspects** – current quality of customer base, potential of customer retention, potential of new customers. Beware of customer concentrations that could be devastating. If the business has a customer base concentrated in one or a few customers it creates a condition some call "too many eggs in one basket."

If you lose one or a few major customers it could sink the ship. This is a danger which should be avoided or fully dealt with in the valuation of the enterprise

» **Facility aspects** – condition, adequacy, assurance of retention, potential for expansion, and productivity of facilities. The retention of facilities at an affordable cost should be assured unless relocating would not cause a costly interruption of the business

» **Industry aspects** – trends, technological advancements, obsolescence, potential growth or decline

14. Documentation

In acquiring a business the closing of the transaction would normally be done in accordance with the existing state law. Some states require closings to be consummated by an attorney. Some require a licensed escrow agent to complete the transaction. Documents should be prepared by or approved by the closing attorney or escrow agent. Most states have Uniform Commercial Code (UCC) laws which require business sale transactions, which are called bulk sale transactions, to be advertised for a specified period of time for the protection of the buyer and any lenders that may have a registered interest in the assets being acquired. Closing documents should be reviewed by an attorney familiar with business sale transactions, even if a closing attorney is not required by your state.

15. Integration

Integration of the buyer of the business with the employees, customers, and vendors is very important to the survival and success of the business. There should be a requirement of the seller to provide transition assistance and participate in the integration process. A period of training and transition assistance is normally included in the transaction in order to provide assurance of a smooth transition of the business to the new owner and to enhance the new owner's success in customer, employee, and vendor retention.

Once you have selected a business with which you feel comfortable, a business you feel that is commensurately priced with its value, and that has good potential for sustainability and growth, you should prepare a business plan to help you and possibly others to consider every aspect of the feasibility of the acquisition.

CHAPTER 6

A Business Plan for Buying a Business

PREPARING A BUSINESS plan is a good practice in the process of buying a business. It can be beneficial in your evaluation of the business and would probably be essential in order to attract investors or lenders. A business plan will help you to understand all of the steps, all of the important considerations in the decision-making process, in order for you to make an informed and rational decision about the business in question.

A business plan usually consists of a complete summary of the business venture, including comprehensive information about you and others who may be involved in managing the enterprise. It should include realistic financial projections from the beginning of the acquisition. It should include a marketing plan explaining how you will retain customers and attract new customers and the volume of business you anticipate from them. It should include a realistic growth plan to enhance profitability. It should include your financial ability, your plan to finance the acquisition, and your plan to provide capital to cover any possible shortfall of earnings initially. It should include a reserve for contingencies to cover any unexpected expenditures which may occur.

A business plan illustration of funding for an acquired company might look something like this:

Sources and Uses of Funds	
Capital:	
Cash in bank	300,000
Bank loan commitment	100,000
Funds from others	50,000
Total funds available	450,000
Acquisition costs:	
Purchase price	300,000
Capital improvements	50,000
Total cost	350,000
Balance of funds:	
Working capital	50,000
Contingency reserve	50,000
Total use of funds	450,000

A BUSINESS PLAN FOR BUYING A BUSINESS

A business plan illustration for the cash flow of the company under consideration might look something like the following chart:

Cash Flow			
	Year 1	Year 2	Year 3
Total Sales	520,000	550,000	620,000
Cost of Sales:			
Beginning Inventory	40,000	50,000	60,000
Materials Purchases	190,000	190,000	200,000
Outside Services	20,000	20,000	20,000
Direct Labor	80,000	90,000	100,000
Ending Inventory	(50,000)	(60,000)	(70,000)
Total Cost of Sales	280,000	290,000	310,000
Gross Profit	240,000	260,000	310,000
Expenses:			
Advertising	5,000	5,000	5,000
Auto	2,000	2,000	2,000
Insurance	8,000	8,000	8,000
Legal & Accounting	2,000	2,000	2,000
Office Expense	4,000	4,000	4,000
Rent	24,000	24,000	24,000
Salary Owner	50,000	50,000	70,000
Salaries & Wages	60,000	66,000	72,000
Taxes, Licenses	4,000	4,000	4,000
Telephone	4,000	4,000	4,000
Utilities	6,000	6,000	6,000
Other	5,000	5,000	5,000
Total Expenses	174,000	180,000	206,000
Cash Flow from Operations	66,000	80,000	104,000
Other Disbursements:			
Purchase Loan Payments	12,000	12,000	12,000
Leasehold Improvements	6,000		
Equipment Purchase		5,000	15,000
Estimated Income Taxes	0	3,000	8,000
Cash Flow	48,000	60,000	69,000

These pro forma cash flow projections reflect a revenue growth of about 6% to 12% annually, improvement of purchasing price of raw materials, reduction of outsourcing and direct labor costs, and increases of gross profit and cash flow. On a purchase price of $350,000 and a total investment of $450,000, the company is projected to produce cash flow of $48,000 the first year with the owner's salary of $50,000, $60,000 the second year with the owner's salary of $50,000, and $69,000 the third year with the owner's salary of $70,000.

Should the company be capable of maintaining or improving cash flow in future years, the return on investment (ROI) would repay the borrowed funds and the initial purchase price in a few years, enable borrowing capacity, and provide funds for expansion.

Bear in mind that the above figures are hypothetical and are illustrated as an example of the way to use the business plan cash flow projections to justify the acquisition cost to the buyer or potential lenders or investors.

A typical business plan would include many features other than a cash flow projection. The other elements included would depend upon the use of the business plan. If it is only for personal analysis of the feasibility of a purchase, the other elements would be less important than if it is being prepared for a potential lender or investor.

Other information that could be included:

- A discussion of the history of the company, when it was founded and by whom
- Historical financial statements, including: balance sheets, income statements, cash flow statements, sources and uses of funds, tax returns for several years
- A description in detail of the products and services provided
- A description, including photos, of the company facilities
- A summary of the competing companies in the industry and area
- A discussion of the customers, including percentages of business that each provides for the company
- A marketing plan explaining the plans for customer retention and future growth of the customer base

- A long term plan for expansion of products, services, or geographical areas

The Business Plan Format

The typical business plan provides sections to describe all of the information that is needed to understand the makeup of the company. The sections should be:

Executive Summary – a snapshot of the business plan and a profile or overview of the company.

Company Description – a more comprehensive description of the products or services the company provides, the markets served, the customer base, the differentiation of the company from competitors.

Market Analysis – a description of the industry, the market, and the competitors.

Organization & Management – a description of the management, the qualifications, the experience, the expertise in the industry in particular and business in general.

Products and Services – a description of the products and services offered by the company.

Marketing and Sales – the present and planned marketing and sales program.

Funding for the Venture – Personal funds, family funds, or planned borrowed funds.

Financial Projections – a detailed income and expense statement and balance sheet with projections for a period of years to support the income and debt service capability required for a viable enterprise.

You can hire a business sale specialist or a business consultant to prepare a business plan for you. You can also find companies online that prepare business plans and/or offer business plan formats for you to prepare your own. The U.S. Small Business Administration (SBA) provides information on preparation of a business plan as well.

A BUSINESS OF YOUR OWN

If you engage a professional to assist you in your acquisition process, you should select a professional willing and able to assist you in this critical step of a comprehensive and diligent selection of a business that will enable you to accomplish your objectives.

Below is an illustration of a brief business plan that could be submitted for the review of potential investors, partners or lenders for a business acquisition. This sample is abbreviated and is merely an example of the information that is important for those who would review it in consideration of an investment or loan for a business venture.

APPAREL MANUFACTURING, INC.

2015 BUSINESS PLAN

OWNER: WILLIAM YOUNG

MAILING ADDRESS: 123 MAIN STREET

ANYWHERE, CA 90000

TELEPHONE: 202-970-3456

EMAIL: WILLIAMYOUNG@EMAIL.COM

Table of Contents

1. **Executive Summary**
   Introduction
   Mission Statement
   Plan for Success

2. **Company Summary**
   Company Ownership
   Management & Staffing
   Company Facilities

3. **Products and Services**
   The Market for Company Products

4. **Manufacturing Facility**

5. **Staffing for the Company**

6. **Funding Plan for the Company**
   Sources and Uses of Funds

7. **Financial Statements**
   Balance Sheet
   Cash Flow Projections

1. Executive Summary

Introduction

The purpose of this business plan is to summarize the business and financial structure and management for the acquisition of **Apparel Manufacturing, Inc.** (the company) and to provide a detailed plan to organize, finance, staff and operate the company successfully and profitably.

The company is located at 123 Main Street, Garment City, CA 90000 in a modern industrial park which is occupied by several other small manufacturing and distribution companies.

The principal company owner will be William Young, who has lengthy experience in the apparel manufacturing industry and has a well-prepared acquisition plan with extensive financial planning to assure a successful new venture.

Mission Statement

The mission of the acquisition of Apparel Manufacturing is to continue the current manufacturing processes, retain the customer base with a productive and efficient manufacturing facility that provides high quality garments for a growing customer base.

Plan for Success

The plan for success includes a continuance of timely service at competitive prices, staying abreast of the latest fashions and the manufacturing techniques required to provide the highest possible quality of merchandise, and upgrading the facilities for enhanced productivity.

2. Company Summary

Company Ownership

The principal owner of Apparel Manufacturing, Inc. will be William Young, 123 Main Street, Garment City, CA 90000 (the CEO).

Management and Staffing

The company shall be managed by the CEO who has the education, experience and management skills to organize and operate the company successfully. The CEO has more than ten years' experience in garment manufacturing. He has some formal education in fashion design and has successfully performed in a management role for other garment manufacturing companies.

Company Facilities

The company plans to continue operations in the present well-equipped facility which has a trained staff of experienced employees. The customer service will be handled by the CEO and an administrative assistant with good people skills and a keen understanding of the business.

The financial projections provided herein have been thoughtfully researched and planned to adequately fund the operation, to maintain the level of profitability that now exists in the company and to provide for growth and expansion, including any required facility improvements.

All funding projections have been planned through research and actual cost estimates of leasehold improvements, fixtures, equipment and inventory.

The financial projections have been prepared with industry research, the owner's management experience and studies of successful competitors in the area.

A BUSINESS PLAN FOR BUYING A BUSINESS

3. Products and Services to be Offered

The company plans to continue the current operations while introducing new items of current fashion trends to enhance the line with a wider variety of fashions.

The Market for the Company's Products

Women's apparel represents a large portion of apparel sales throughout the country. Trendy fashion for teens and young ladies represents a large portion of retail sales of female apparel. By focusing on the company's chosen age group and styles, the company owner believes he has selected a segment of the market which offers the best chance of building a steady and profitable business in the shortest length of time.

The company plans to increase distribution by marketing the products through advertising in local newspapers and direct mailing to local market areas. The popular retail center provides a steady local clientele which currently visits the facility for other retail establishments.

The company plans to launch the store with a well-advertised grand opening and welcoming sales that will attract thousands of new customers to the facility.

4. Manufacturing Facility

The facility consists of a leased, well-equipped garment manufacturing plant of 5,000 square feet with an option to increase the space as adjacent space becomes available. The space layout is designed to provide 4,000 square feet for manufacturing, 500 square feet of office and storage space and additional space for restrooms, employee lunchroom, and employee break areas.

5. Staffing and Employment Policies

Management and staffing shall include:

A BUSINESS OF YOUR OWN

» The owner as general manager
» A shop foreman that is presently employed at the facility
» Five employees as full-time machine operators
» Three employees for material handling, shipping, and receiving
» One full-time salesperson with garment sales experience
» One clerical employee for office duties.

6. Funding Plan for the Company

The company plans to arrange funding for the acquisition, including any upgrades to equipment, leasehold improvements, inventory and working capital, through owner's personal funds and local bank financing, with possible assistance from the Small Business Administration, if required. The SBA has been contacted for information about plans available and application instructions.

The following table outlines the funding requirements:

Sources and Uses of Funds	
Capital:	
Cash in bank	300,000
Bank loan commitment	100,000
Family funds pledge	50,000
Total funds available	**450,000**
Acquisition costs:	
Purchase price	300,000
Capital improvements	50,000
Total cost	**350,000**
Balance of funds:	
Working capital	50,000
Contingency reserve	50,000
Total use of funds	**450,000**

7. Financial Statements

Some examples of beginning and projected financial statements are illustrated below:

Balance Sheet

Apparel Manufacturing, Inc. Beginning Balance Sheet	
Assets:	
Current Assets:	
Cash in Bank	150,000
Accounts Receivable	
Inventory	50,000
Total Current Assets	200,000
Long-term Assets:	
Furniture, Fixtures & Equipment	150,000
Goodwill	100,000
Total Assets	**450,000**
Liabilities & Owner's Equity	
Current Liabilities:	
Accounts Payable	
Loan Payable in less than 12 months	12,000
Long Term Liabilities:	
Loan Payable in excess of 12 months	138,000
Capital:	
Paid-in Capital	300,000
Retained Earnings	
Total Liabilities & Owner's Equity	**450,000**

Cash Flow Projections

Cash Flow			
	Year 1	Year 2	Year 3
Total Sales	520,000	550,000	620,000
Cost of Sales:			
Beginning Inventory	40,000	50,000	60,000
Materials Purchases	190,000	190,000	200,000
Outside Services	20,000	20,000	20,000
Direct Labor	80,000	90,000	100,000
Ending Inventory	(50,000)	(60,000)	(70,000)
Total Cost of Sales	280,000	290,000	310,000
Gross Profit	240,000	260,000	310,000
Expenses:			
Advertising	5,000	5,000	5,000
Auto	2,000	2,000	2,000
Insurance	8,000	8,000	8,000
Legal & Accounting	2,000	2,000	2,000
Office Expense	4,000	4,000	4,000
Rent	24,000	24,000	24,000
Salary Owner	50,000	50,000	70,000
Salaries & Wages	60,000	66,000	72,000
Taxes, Licenses	4,000	4,000	4,000
Telephone	4,000	4,000	4,000
Utilities	6,000	6,000	6,000
Other	5,000	5,000	5,000
Total Expenses	174,000	180,000	206,000
Cash Flow from Operations	66,000	80,000	104,000
Other Disbursements:			
Purchase Loan Payments	12,000	12,000	12,000
Leasehold Improvements	6,000		
Equipment Purchase		5,000	15,000
Estimated Income Taxes	0	3,000	8,000
Cash Flow	48,000	60,000	69,000

CHAPTER 7

Starting a New Business

STARTING A NEW business can be a challenging and stressful endeavor, but it has been done millions of times and is done many times every day. You can do it successfully if you follow the essential steps that are beneficial to assure a successful enterprise. Success requires careful planning, diligence, hard work and a little luck along the way. We have all heard the saying, *the harder I work, the luckier I get*. In other words, when I work hard and smart, the luck follows.

The following are some essential steps and some essential questions you should address in starting a business.

Identify your objectives

What are your objectives for starting a business? Earning a living, being your own boss, building some equity value, assuming more control of your future income, pursuing a business you desire? Are you interested in the long term or a short term venture? Are you truly interested in being a successful entrepreneur and building something meaningful and lasting, something to which you will be dedicated and invest your time and money and perhaps the money of others? Are you willing to forgo employment opportunities so that you can build a company of your own?

Decide the type of business you desire.

Do you have expertise in any type of business that you wish to pursue? Is there a particular type of business that you desire? Are you interested in manufacturing, retail establishments, wholesale supply, personal services, construction services, automotive services, food and beverage services, internet services, marketing services, accounting, insurance services, entertainment services?

Determine the capital requirements.

Determine the facilities required for your business. Can you start it at home and build it from there? Will you require a factory, warehouse, retail space, office space, vacant property? What size space will you need? What will be the space and rent requirements for your required facilities?

How much income will you require to sustain the lifestyle for you and your family? How much capital can you invest in a business? Do you have any borrowing capacity from family or other sources? If so, what would be the repayment terms?

How long can you sustain yourself without any income from your new business? Have you prepared an accurate budget of your living expenses in order to determine the period of time that you can survive financially without income from your new business?

What leasehold improvements will be required? Will you need to build out offices, kitchens, retail displays, warehousing facilities, or customer service accommodations?

What office equipment, factory machinery, service benches, showcases, service counters, storage racks, or interior furnishings will be needed?

How much inventory will be needed to provide a comfortable level of supply to fill customer orders in a timely manner?

How much working capital will be required? Will you be carrying accounts receivable for your customers? Will you have any accounts payable terms from your suppliers or will you be on a cash basis initially? How much will your initial payroll be? What is the total of all expenses requiring payment prior to your receipt of customer payments? All of the above will have an impact on your working capital, so this determination will establish your initial financial requirement.

What insurance protection will you need initially? Will you need casualty insurance on your facilities, liability insurance on your operation, product liability, or workers' compensation insurance? Will there be payment terms for these policies or must they be paid in advance?

Consider the employees and expertise required.

What type of employees will you need? Will you need a chef, a mechanic, a machinist, a salesperson, an internet technician, a sales clerk, an office assistant? Will employees with special skills be difficult to attain? What will be that cost initially? What will be the total of employee wages and payroll taxes prior to anticipated receipt of customer payments?

Consider the development of customers for your business.

How will you build your customer base? Do you have customers on hand when you start or will you be starting without any clientele? How long will it take to develop customers? How can you provide something that will encourage potential customers to do business with you instead of the company they are doing business with now? Will you be price competitive; can your new business survive by underpricing the competition?

Consider the likelihood of continued growth of your business.

What is the likelihood of your new business continuing to grow? Is there an abundance of potential customers in your service area? Can you attract them away from their current supplier with better service, a better product, or better pricing? Can you sustain and grow your business under your perceived pricing or service structure?

A BUSINESS OF YOUR OWN

The above list of considerations is not all-inclusive. They are all important but do not all apply to every venture. You should prepare your own list of considerations in order to do a comprehensive study and make a positive decision about the business that you intend to found and build into your own successful enterprise.

Not unlike buying a business, preparation of a business plan will help you to consider all of the critical elements that should be included in your feasibility study.

CHAPTER 8

A Business Plan for Starting a Business

AS WE DISCUSSED in the previous section on buying a business, preparing a business plan is a good practice in the process of starting a business. It can be beneficial in determining the practicality, the requirements for achieving success, the total investment required. A business plan would probably be essential in order to attract investors or lenders, either initially or at some other point, so the importance cannot be overstated.

A business plan for a start-up business usually consists of a complete summary of your intended business venture, including comprehensive information about you and others who may be involved in managing the enterprise. It should include realistic financial projections from the beginning of the start-up. It should include a marketing plan explaining how you will attract customers and the volume of business you anticipate from them. It will include a realistic growth plan to reach profitability. It will include your personal financial capability, your plan to finance the start-up venture, and your plan to provide capital to cover any shortfall of earnings over expenses initially. It should include a reserve for contingencies to cover any unexpected expenditures which may be required.

A BUSINESS OF YOUR OWN

A business plan illustration of funding for an acquired company should be realistic. Don't fudge the numbers to make the bottom line work. Making unreasonable projections from unreasonable expectations, if not accomplished, will make future projections deemed unreasonable by lenders or investors.

A business plan illustration for funding might look something like this:

Sources and Uses of Funds	
Capital:	
Cash in Bank	200,000
Bank Loan Commitment	100,000
Family Funds Pledge	50,000
Total funds available	**350,000**
Acquisition costs:	
Furniture, Fixtures & Equipment	125,000
Inventory	50,000
Leasehold Improvements	75,000
Working capital	50,000
Contingency reserve	50,000
Total use of funds	**350,000**

A BUSINESS PLAN FOR STARTING A BUSINESS

A business plan illustration for the cash flow of the company under consideration might look something like this:

Cash Flow			
	Year 1	Year 2	Year 3
Total Sales	350,000	450,000	550,000
Cost of Sales:			
Beginning Inventory	50,000	60,000	60,000
Materials Purchases	150,000	190,000	250,000
Sales Salaries	60,000	70,000	80,000
Ending Inventory	(60,000)	(60,000)	(70,000)
Total Cost of Sales	200,000	260,000	320,000
Gross Profit	150,000	190,000	230,000
Expenses:			
Advertising	5,000	10,000	10,000
Auto	5,000	5,000	5,000
Insurance	8,000	8,000	10,000
Legal & Accounting	5,000	5,000	5,000
Office Expense	3,000	5,000	5,000
Rent	48,000	48,000	54,000
Salary - Owner	50,000	60,000	70,000
Taxes, Licenses	1,000	2,000	2,000
Telephone	3,000	3,000	3,000
Utilities	5,000	5,000	6,000
Other	5,000	8,000	10,000
Total Expenses	138,000	159,000	180,000
Cash Flow from Operations	12,000	31,000	50,000
Other Disbursements:			
Loan Payments	12,000	12,000	12,000
Leasehold Improvements		5,000	5,000
Equipment Purchase		3,000	
Cash Flow	0	11,000	33,000

This example of pro forma cash flow projections reflects a revenue growth of about 25% annually, which provides increases of gross profit and cash flow. On a total investment of $350,000, the company is projected to provide increasing income for the owner and retire the

69

borrowed funds within a few years. The projected increases in sales and profits should be substantiated with detailed promotional planning and convincing evidence of success in other similar operations.

Bear in mind that these figures are hypothetical and are illustrated as an example of the way to use the business plan cash flow projections to justify the acquisition cost to the buyer or potential lenders or investors.

A typical business plan for a start-up business should include many other features other than a cash flow projection. The comprehensiveness of the other elements included would depend upon the use of the business plan. If it is for personal analysis of the feasibility of a purchase it can be essential in emphasizing the realities of income and expenses for the owner of the venture. If it is being prepared for a potential lender or investor, care should be taken to qualify any assumptions of income and expenses and to emphasize that the projections are based upon the best knowledge of the preparer or upon whatever sources the estimates are established.

Other information that could be included:

- A description in detail of the products and services to be provided
- A description of the suppliers for products provided
- A description of the planned company facilities
- A summary of the competing companies in the industry and area
- A discussion of the customers and a supporting plan to attract customers
- A marketing plan explaining the plans for a continuing growth of the customer base
- A long term plan for expansion of products, services, or geographical areas
- And above all, information expressing your ability to fund, promote, and operate the business in a profitable manner.

Illustrated below is an example of a brief business plan of a start-up company:

Trendy Fashions

Business Plan

July 1, 2015

Owner: Beverly Jones

Mailing Address: 123 Main Street

Anywhere, CA 90000

Telephone: 800-900-1000

Email: Beverly@email.com

Table of Contents

1. **Executive Summary**
   Introduction
   Mission Statement
   Plan for Success

2. **Company Summary**
   Company Ownership
   Management and Staffing
   Company Facilities

3. **Products and Services**
   Product Types and Styles
   Pricing of Product Lines

4. **Market Analysis**
   Market Segmentation
   Target Market
   Marketing strategy
   Sales forecast
   Sales forecast table
   Sales strategy

5. **Financial Plan**
   Business Financial Plan
   Investments and Funding
   Initial Balance Sheet Projection
   Initial Cash Flow Projection
   Profit and Loss Projection

1. Executive Summary

Introduction

The purpose of this business plan is to summarize the business operation, financial structure, and management strategy for **Trendy Fashions** ("the company") and to provide a detailed plan to organize, finance, staff and operate a successful and profitable company.

The company shall be located at the Main Street Fashion Center, 456 Grand Avenue, Fashion City, CA 90000. Main Street Fashion Center has been a well-established center for more than ten years, located on a major thoroughfare in Fashion City.

Main Street Fashion Center is currently occupied by twenty-four retail stores offering apparel for teenage and young adult females. The fashion styles that the company plans to offer are not now being offered by other retail shops in the center.

The company owner, Beverly Jones, has lengthy experience in the apparel industry and has planned this start-up retail store with financial planning for a successful new venture.

Mission Statement

The mission of Trendy Fashions is to create an attractive retail store that provides a pleasant shopping experience for its customers with personalized service, enticing displays and current trends in fashions for teenage and young adult females.

Pricing of merchandise is meant to offer good value at a reasonable price, competitive with other area retailers of similar merchandise.

Plan for Success

The plan for success includes offering the right fashions at the right price for the area, staying abreast of the latest trends in teen and young adult fashions, offering modeling events with sale pricing to attract a large customer base and to build loyalty with a reputation of reliability for providing personal attention and satisfaction.

2. Company Summary

Company Ownership

The owner of Trendy Fashions will be Beverly Jones, 123 Main Street, Fashion City, CA 90000 (the owner). Beverly Jones has the education, experience and management skills to organize and operate the company successfully.

Management and Staffing

Beverly Jones will provide general management of the store. Beverly has more than ten years experience in retail sales of fashion for girls and ladies. She has some formal education in fashion design and has successfully performed in a management role for several small and large retailers of fashions for women.

An assistance manager with retail management experience in women's apparel will be hired to assist Beverly Jones. Either Beverly Jones or the assistant manager will be on duty at all times during open hours.

Two full-time and three part-time salespersons with retail experience will be hired to provide timely and quality service for customers at all times.

Company Facilities

The planned facility consists of a retail store front in the Main Street Fashion Center. The company has received an option to lease a well-located space of 1,500 square feet in a good traffic area of the center. The space layout is designed to provide 1,200 square feet of retail space, 200 square feet of office and storage space and additional space for restrooms and dressing rooms.

The interior is to be finished with clothing racks along the side walls and table high display areas in the center areas with ample walk space throughout. The walls will be finished with modern style wallpaper with bright colors. The floor will be hardwood.

There will be a sound system for low grade background music. The cashiering station will be near the exit door and will be equipped with a state-of-the-art cashiering system.

The company plans to provide an attractively designed facility with an inventory of high quality and trendy merchandise with a middle income price point. The customer service focus will be efficient and friendly personal service in order to attract a steady and solid flow of loyal and satisfied customers.

3. Products and Services

Product Types and Styles

The company plans to offer a trendy selection of fashions for teens and young adults, including pants, skirts, blouses, pullovers, sweaters, tee shirts and casual footwear. Items selected will be those for which the company can receive supplier assurance of non-competition at the company's location by any competitors.

Pricing of Product Lines

The company plans to offer products in price ranges to meet the typical clothing budget guidelines of the service area. The center is located in an upper middle class area of the city and products will be priced accordingly. Pricing of products in neighborhood stores will be studied prior to selection of product lines in order to be competitive with area stores.

4. Market Analysis

The Market for the Company's Products

Women's apparel represents a large portion of apparel sales throughout the country. Fashions for teens and young ladies represent a large portion of retail sales of women's apparel. By focusing on the company's chosen age group and styles the company owner believes she has selected a segment of the market which offers her the best chance of building a steady and profitable business in the shortest length of time.

Marketing Strategy

The company plans to market the products through advertising in local newspapers and direct mailing to local market areas. The popular retail center provides a steady local clientele which currently visits the facility for other retail establishments.

The company plans to launch the store with a well-advertised grand opening including enticing sales that will attract thousands of new customers to the facility.

5. Financial Plan

Business Financial Plan

The company plans to arrange funding for the leasehold improvements, furnishings, display fixtures, lease costs, organizational formation costs, inventory and working capital through the owner's personal funds and local bank financing, with possible assistance from the Small Business Administration, if required. The SBA has been contacted for information about plans available and application instructions.

The financial projections provided herein have been thoughtfully researched and planned to adequately fund the operation, to reach a level of profitability within the first year of operation, and to provide for growth and expansion within three years of operation.

All funding projections have been planned through research and actual cost estimates of leasehold improvements, fixtures, equipment and inventory.

The financial projections have been prepared with industry research, the owner's management experience and studies of successful competitors in the area.

Below are detailed illustrations supporting the financial plan, including Sources and Uses of Funds, Balance Sheet, and Cash Flow Statement:

Investments and Funding

Sources and Uses of Funds	
Capital:	
Cash in Bank	200,000
Bank Loan Commitment	100,000
Family Funds Pledge	50,000
Total funds available	**350,000**
Acquisition costs:	
Furniture, Fixtures & Equipment	125,000
Inventory	50,000
Leasehold Improvements	75,000
Working capital	50,000
Contingency reserve	50,000
Total use of funds	**350,000**

Balance Sheet

Trendy Fashions Beginning Balance Sheet	
Assets:	
Cash in Bank	100,000
Accounts Receivable	
Inventory	50,000
Total Current Assets	**150,000**
Long-term Assets	
Leasehold Improvements	75,000
Furniture, Fixtures & Equipment	125,000
Total Long-term Assets:	**200,000**
Total Asets	**350,000**
Liabilities & Owner's Equity	
Current Liabilities:	
Accounts Payable	
Loan Payable in less than 12 months	12,000
Long Term Liabilities:	
Loan Payable in excess of 12 months	138,000
Capital:	
Paid-in Capital	200,000
Total Liabilities & Owner's Equity	**350,000**

Cash Flow Statement

Cash Flow			
	Year 1	Year 2	Year 3
Total Sales	350,000	450,000	550,000
Cost of Sales:			
Beginning Inventory	50,000	60,000	60,000
Materials Purchases	150,000	190,000	250,000
Sales Salaries	60,000	70,000	80,000
Ending Inventory	(60,000)	(60,000)	(70,000)
Total Cost of Sales	200,000	260,000	320,000
Gross Profit	150,000	190,000	230,000
Expenses:			
Advertising	5,000	10,000	10,000
Auto	5,000	5,000	5,000
Insurance	8,000	8,000	10,000
Legal & Accounting	5,000	5,000	5,000
Office Expense	3,000	5,000	5,000
Rent	48,000	48,000	54,000
Salary - Owner	50,000	60,000	70,000
Taxes, Licenses	1,000	2,000	2,000
Telephone	3,000	3,000	3,000
Utilities	5,000	5,000	6,000
Other	5,000	8,000	10,000
Total Expenses	138,000	159,000	180,000
Cash Flow from Operations	12,000	31,000	50,000
Other Disbursements:			
Loan Payments	12,000	12,000	12,000
Leasehold Improvements		5,000	5,000
Equipment Purchase		3,000	
Cash Flow	0	11,000	33,000

CHAPTER 9

Financing Alternatives

Financing sources for a business acquisition

Financing for a business acquisition can be available from various sources. It could be provided by a direct bank loan, a bank loan with a Small Business Administration (SBA) guarantee, seller financing when acquiring a company whereby the seller accepts a portion of the purchase over an extended period, or financing by venture capital lenders, or other investors.

Bank loans

A bank loan for the acquisition of a small business is a possible source of financing. Although banks are rarely in the start-up loan business, as they typically consider such ventures as high-risk, they are sometimes a source for business acquisitions. In order for a bank to lend for the acquisition of a small business, the bank would require the business to have undisputed financial records reflecting good historical earnings and reliable forecasts of future earnings with adequate capacity to service the bank loan without interrupting the cash flow of the business. In most cases the bank loan would not be granted without additional collateral, such as home equity. A bank would typically not finance a small business acquisition without an SBA guarantee for a major portion of the loan. SBA guarantees are readily available but require stringent qualification of the buyer, including earnings records or evidence of the assurance of future earnings similar to those required by the bank. Although SBA does not loan to businesses directly, SBA programs have facilitated the necessary capital for many businesses over the last 50 years and remain today as a source of such financing, sometimes the only source.

Seller financing

Many business sale transactions are consummated with some financing by the seller of the business. The seller sometimes carries back a portion of the purchase price for a period of years as a seller note or carry-back loan, to ease the financing process for the buyer. Many sale transactions simply could not be completed without some seller financing. Banks making direct loans or loans with SBA guarantees often require the seller to carry some portion of the sale price in order to provide assurance of the seller's confidence in the buyer's ability to manage the business, as well as the long-term viability of the business.

Loans from family members or friends

Many business acquisitions are financed by venture capital, loans from private lenders such as venture investors, family members, or friends. This lending source saves many business sale transactions. The private lenders are usually required to subordinate their loans to any bank or SBA financing, which would require the private lender to pay off the commercial lender in order to foreclose for nonpayment. Therefore such loans can be a source of strained relationships amongst family or friends and the terms can be challenging for the private lender to accept.

Financing sources for business start-ups

Like business acquisitions, financing for a business start-up is sometimes provided by a direct bank loan, a bank loan with an SBA guarantee, seller financing, or financing by venture capital lenders, friends, or family members. A start-up business would generally undergo more scrutiny and less chance of approval of a loan application, simply due to the lack of positive operating results, the risk of failure, and the cost and difficulty of receiving satisfactory repayment through foreclosure from a failed venture.

Bank loans

Like a business acquisition, a bank loan for a business start-up is a possible source of financing, although banks are not really a good source for that type of loan due to the risk level. In order for a bank to lend for the start-up of a small business, the bank would require substantial financial projections, a comprehensive business plan, evidence of the capability of the business owner to manage the business, and adequate collateral to cover the loan or a loan guarantee from SBA. Although SBA does not loan directly to businesses, SBA programs have facilitated the necessary capital for many business start-ups over the last 50 years and remain today as a source of such financing, sometimes the only source, but many more such loan guarantees are requested than are granted. The SBA is generally as stringent as a bank in approving a loan guarantee application.

Banks that make loans for business ventures generally focus on the Six Cs of Credit:

- Character – the character of the business owner signing the promissory note and the assurance of repayment of the indebtedness
- Capital – the capital the owner is investing in the business venture
- Cash Flow – the ability of the operation to generate sufficient income for timely financial commitments and servicing of loan payments
- Collateral – sufficient collateral to secure the loan upon default of repayment

- Coverage – insurance on loan collateral and/or on the life of borrower
- Conditions – the industry conditions, risks of failure, competitive conditions, and business cycles that could affect income and repayment

Loans from family members or friends

Many start-up businesses are financed by loans from family or friends, but like business acquisitions, these private lenders usually must subordinate their loans to future bank or SBA financing, which would require the private lender to pay off the commercial lender in order to foreclose for non-payment. Therefore such loans can be a source of strained relationships amongst family or friends and the terms challenging for the private lender to accept – falling under the category of venture capital.

SBA Loan Programs

SBA programs play a big role in business acquisitions and business start-ups. Without the SBA programs many of them would fail for lack of financing. It is a good idea to have some understanding of the programs, requirements, and terms available.

The most applicable program for small business start-ups and acquisitions is the 7(a) program.

Under the 7(a) program you can use the loan proceeds to establish a new business or to assist in the acquisition, operation, or expansion of an existing business.

This program also permits the use of funding, as follows:

- to provide long-term working capital for operational expenses, accounts payable or inventory
- for short-term working capital needs,
- for construction financing and exporting,
- for revolving funds based on the value of existing inventory and receivables,

- to purchase equipment, machinery, furniture, fixtures, supplies or materials,
- to purchase real estate, including land and buildings,
- to construct a new building or renovate an existing building,
- to refinance existing business debt.

The SBA's loan programs are generally intended to encourage longer term small-business financing. However, actual loan maturities are based on the ability to repay, the purpose of the loan proceeds and the useful life of the assets financed. Maximum loan maturities have been established: twenty-five years for real estate, up to ten years for equipment, and generally up to seven years for working capital. Short-term loans and revolving lines of credit are also available through the SBA to help small businesses meet their short-term and cyclical working capital needs.

The SBA expects every 7(a) loan to be fully secured, but the SBA will not decline a request to guarantee a loan if the only unfavorable factor is insufficient collateral, provided all available collateral is offered. This means every SBA loan is to be secured by all available assets (both business and personal) until the recovery value equals the loan amount or until all assets have been pledged (to the extent that they are reasonably available). Personal guarantees are required from all owners of 20 percent or more of the equity of the business, and lenders can require personal guarantees of owners with less than 20 percent ownership. Liens on personal assets of the principals may be required.

The specific terms of SBA loans are negotiated between a borrower and an SBA-approved lender. In general, the following provisions apply to all SBA 7(a) loans.

7(a) loans have a maximum loan amount of $5 million. SBA does not set a minimum loan amount.

Loans guaranteed by the SBA are assessed a guarantee fee. This fee is based on the loan's maturity and the dollar amount guaranteed, not the total loan amount. The lender initially pays the guaranty fee

FINANCING ALTERNATIVES

and they have the option to pass that expense on to the borrower at closing. The funds to reimburse the lender can be included in the overall loan proceeds.

On loans under $150,000 the fees are zero percent. On any loan greater than $150,000 with a maturity of one year or shorter, the fee is 0.25 percent of the guaranteed portion of the loan. On loans with maturities of more than one year, the normal fee is 3 percent of the SBA-guaranteed portion on loans of $150,000 to $700,000, and 3.5 percent on loans of more than $700,000. There is also an additional fee of 0.25 percent on any guaranteed portion of more than $1 million.

The actual interest rate for a 7(a) loan guaranteed by the SBA is negotiated between the applicant and lender and subject to the SBA maximums. Both fixed and variable interest rate structures are available. The maximum rate is composed of two parts, a base rate and an allowable spread. There are three acceptable base rates (A prime rate published in a daily national newspaper*, London Interbank One Month Prime plus 3 percent and an SBA Peg Rate).

Lenders are allowed to add an additional spread to the base rate to arrive at the final rate. For loans with maturities of shorter than seven years, the maximum spread will be no more than 2.25 percent. For loans with maturities of seven years or more, the maximum spread will be 2.75 percent. The spread on loans of less than $50,000 and loans processed through Express procedures have higher maximums.

SBA can guarantee as much as 85 percent on loans of up to $150,000 and 75 percent on loans of more than $150,000. SBA's maximum exposure amount is $3,750,000. Thus, if a business receives an SBA-guaranteed loan for $5 million, the maximum guarantee to the lender will be $3,750,000 or 75%. SBA Express loans have a maximum guarantee set at 50 percent.

Microloan Program

The Microloan program provides loans up to $50,000 to help small businesses and certain not-for-profit childcare centers start up and expand.

A BUSINESS OF YOUR OWN

The U.S. Small Business Administration provides funds to specially designated intermediary lenders, which are nonprofit community-based organizations with experience in lending as well as management and technical assistance. These intermediaries administer the Microloan program for eligible borrowers.

Each intermediary lender has its own lending and credit requirements. Generally, intermediaries require some type of collateral as well as the personal guarantee of the business owner.

Microloans can be used for working capital, inventory or supplies, furniture or fixtures, machinery or equipment.

The maximum repayment term allowed for an SBA microloan is six years.

Interest rates vary, depending on the intermediary lender and costs to the intermediary from the U.S. Treasury. Generally, these rates will be between 8 and 13 percent.

CHAPTER **10**

Introduction to Franchises

MANY FIRST TIME business owners choose to avail themselves of the products, services, and processes of established companies who utilize franchising for expansion. The franchising company, the franchisor, provides their established brand name and business plan to the new business owner, the franchisee, who meets their requirements of personal ability and availability of investment capital.

The U.S. Census Bureau reports that in 2007 franchising accounted for more than 10% of total U.S. businesses, and approximately 15% of total sales and total workforce in the U.S. Franchising has proven to be a successful method of business ownership for the franchisee and a successful method of business expansion for the franchisor.

Franchising is an important aspect in the nation's economy in the creation and maintenance of jobs and distribution of goods and services. It provides opportunities for the parent company, the franchisor, to expand by utilizing the capital and ambition of new entrepreneurs, the franchisees.

In the 2007 study, limited-service fast food restaurants, had the highest number of franchise establishments, followed by gas stations with convenience stores.

New car dealers led in sales volume for franchise establishments, followed by gas stations with convenience stores and limited-service restaurants.

87

Sales for franchise establishments in the diet weight loss centers industry represented a majority of all sales for that industry, behind new car dealers and limited service restaurants.

Limited-service restaurants also had the third highest percentage of franchise establishments compared with all establishments within that industry, surpassed only by new car dealers and private mail centers.

Automobile manufacturers established dealerships to market their vehicles and provide service facilities, almost from the inception of the auto industry. Some of the early brands that were mass-produced and available in the early 20th century were Ford, General Motors, Chrysler, Studebaker, Nash, and Hudson. The auto dealer for a given brand had exclusive rights to sell the automobiles of the manufacturer in certain states or locales and was required to operate under specific rules and operating procedures established by the manufacturer. The dealer was also responsible for maintaining a factory approved service facility to serve the vehicle owners.

Becoming an automobile dealer has always required considerable initial capital and automobile business experience. The major automobile companies often provide financing for new dealers for the purchase of auto inventories and acquisition of sales and service facilities.

Many food companies have expanded by the franchising of retail grocery locations as well as fast food locations. The early days of food franchising established such names as: McDonalds, Hardee's, Shakey's Pizza, Kentucky Fried Chicken, Dunkin Donuts, Pizza Hut, Denny's, Taco Bell, Arby's, Burger King, Krispy Kreme, and many others.

Franchising is now used for expansion in many industries in which distribution or services can be performed on a localized basis by private entrepreneurs, without the necessity of the parent company owning and operating a network of local operations with the facilities and staff to market their products. Franchising enables manufacturers, distributors, and service providers to expand more rapidly by engaging franchisees, who provide sales and service operations with leasehold improvements, working capital, and inventory. The franchisee also provides the hiring, training, and supervision of employees to operate the locations.

The Process of Franchising

Typically the franchisee pays an initial franchise fee for the right to establish a facility and operate under the name of the franchisor or the right to sell the franchisor's products or services. The franchisee then generally pays an ongoing franchise fee based on sales or profitability of the operation or is required to purchase all merchandise directly from the franchisor.

The franchisor provides the product or service, the business plan, operating procedures, goodwill of the established successful brand name, and generally provides ongoing training, upgrading of products or services, and advertising campaigns.

Other early franchisors that we all recognize include: AAMCO Transmission, Midas Muffler, Service Master, Budget Car Rental, Dollar Car Rental, and Sir Speedy Printing.

Other franchise type arrangements include those in the hospitality industry with names such as: Hilton Hotels, Sheraton Hotels, Ramada Inns, Marriott Hotels, Hyatt Hotels and many smaller motel chains. Some of these facilities have been operated by the principal company and some operated under types of franchise agreements, with the parent company providing brand name, signage, reservation services, and training, among other services, and establishing strict operating procedures and standards of service.

Insurance companies have historically operated similarly under broker or agent relationships. These relationships are similar in terms to franchise or operating agreements. The broker or agent sometimes represents the company's insurance offerings exclusively or sometimes along with other lines of business. Some insurance companies engage an exclusive broker or agent for a specific territory, some engage multiple brokers in overlapping territories. Names of note in

A BUSINESS OF YOUR OWN

this industry would include: State Farm Insurance Company, Farmers Insurance Company, Allstate Insurance, Mercury Insurance and many others. In representing an insurance company, a broker or agent typically deals with the insured party, takes the application for insurance, and forwards it to the insurance company for acceptance. The parent company would typically accept payment of the premium and pay a commission to the broker or agent.

CHAPTER **11**

Franchise History

THIS SECTION PROVIDES details of the founding and operations of some of the longest established franchising companies and some of the terms of franchise agreements. This will give you an understanding of how franchising works and some of the benefits and restrictions of the relationship of franchisor and franchisee.

Krispy Kreme - Krispy Kreme is a restaurant service company that serves coffee and donuts. Krispy Kreme was established in 1937 by Vernon Rudolf after he bought a Kentucky based donut shop that was previously owned by a French chef. He got the company's assets and rights to the secret donut recipe. The company is a branded specialty retailer and reports that it produces over 3 million donuts each day. On top of operating stores, Krispy Kreme sells the doughnuts in convenience stores, retail outlets and supermarkets. The company also serves espresso drinks and coffee.

Krispy Kreme potential franchisees must be qualified to run a successful establishment, be able to raise the necessary capital, and demonstrate that the market area will support a new retail outlet. Krispy Kreme headquarters is now in North Carolina and is now owned by Beatrice Foods.

They claim various benefits that you can get by running a Krispy Kreme franchise. Krispy Kreme claims to offer a successful concept of services and products. They claim that there is minimal risk of business failure in view of the support that is provided by the franchisor. The franchisees are assisted in selecting the right location for their business. They are also provided with recipes for the new products, new technology and assistance in marketing.

The franchise fee for Krispy Kreme is reported to be $9,500 with some financing available.

McDonald's - In 1940 Dick and Mack McDonald opened McDonald's Bar-B-Que at Fourteenth and E Streets in San Bernardino, California as a drive-in restaurant with carhops. They operated it as such until 1948 when they closed, remodeled, and reopened as McDonald's Famous Hamburgers. Their advertising was: "Buy them by the bag."

Their success is widespread. They now have 36,000 locations, 80% of them are franchised. They operate in 100 countries, and have 69 million customers per day.

McDonald's is a family of over 3,000 owner/operators. McDonald's is committed to franchising as a predominant way of doing business—and claim to be the premier franchise business in the world.

Acquiring a Franchise:

Most owner/operators enter the system by purchasing an existing restaurant, either from McDonald's or from a McDonald's owner/operator. A small number of new operators enter the system by purchasing a new restaurant.

The financial requirements vary depending on the method of acquisition. An initial down payment is required when you purchase a new restaurant (40% of the total cost) or an existing restaurant (25% of the total cost). The down payment must come from non-borrowed personal resources, which include cash on hand; securities, bonds, and debentures; vested profit sharing; and business or real estate equity, exclusive of a personal residence.

Generally, they require a minimum of $750,000 of non-borrowed personal resources to consider a new franchisee. Individuals with additional funds may be better prepared for additional or multi-restaurant opportunities.

They require that the buyer pay a minimum of 25% cash as a down payment toward the purchase of a restaurant. The remaining balance of the purchase price may be financed for a period of no more than seven years.

During the term of the franchise, the franchisee pays McDonald's the following fees:

Service fee: a monthly fee based upon the restaurant's sales performance (currently a service fee of 4.0% of monthly sales).

Rent: a monthly base rent or percentage rent that is a percentage of monthly sales.

Shakey's Pizza Parlor - The history of Shakey's Pizza Parlor began in 1954, when Sherwood "Shakey" Johnson opened the first Shakey's Pizza Parlor in a remodeled grocery store on 57th and J Street in Sacramento, California. Originally established as "Ye Public House" for pizza & beer, Johnson had a passion for Dixieland jazz and added live ragtime music, with banjos and pianos throughout his expanding franchise. The concept caught on. The Shakey's name became synonymous with the great pizza along with slogans such as "You'll have fun at Shakey's, also pizza," and "You can feed your face at any old place, but you can warm your heart at Shakey's." For 60 years, Shakey's has provided fun, food, and music for pizza lovers.

Terms and specifications for Shakey's franchisees:

- Facility size: 4,500 – 5,000 square feet
- Family fast casual franchise featuring a wide variety of specialty pizzas, golden fried chicken, signature Mojo® potatoes and the famous Bunch of Lunch® Buffet.
- Seating 180-230 guests
- Trade area 70,000 minimum
- Investment $850k – 1.2m
- Stand alone, end cap or conversion

A BUSINESS OF YOUR OWN

Kentucky Fried Chicken - Based in Louisville, KY, KFC Corporation claims to be the franchisor of the world's most popular chicken restaurant chain, specializing in Original Recipe, Extra Crispy, Kentucky Grilled Chicken and Extra Crispy Strips with home-style sides, Hot Wings and freshly made chicken sandwiches. KFC has been serving customers complete, freshly prepared, family meals since Colonel Harland Sanders founded the concept in 1952.

They claim to be famous for the Original Recipe fried chicken, which is made with the same secret blend of 11 herbs and spices Colonel Sanders perfected more than a half century ago.

The KFC system serves more than 12 million customers each day in more than 115 countries and territories around the world. KFC operates more than 17,000 restaurants in the Unites States and internationally. KFC's parent company is Yum! Brands, Inc., the world's largest restaurant company in terms of system restaurants, with more than 40,000 locations in more than 130 countries and territories and employing more than one million associates. Yum! is ranked number 201 on the Fortune 500 List, with revenues exceeding $13 billion in 2012.

Franchising Terms:

- Successful business ownership experience
- $1,500,000 net worth, $750,000 liquid assets
- Minimum credit score of 700
- No bankruptcy or litigation history
- Reputation and referrals
- Guarantee franchise agreement obligations
- Hands on in day to day operations

AAMCO Transmission - AAMCO claims that one of the biggest positives in partnering with a nationally known brand with a 50-year history of expertise and customer trust is that the groundwork is already laid. AAMCO states that they have spent decades establishing a preeminent brand, and franchisees benefit from that legacy the day they open their doors.

Though transmission work still generates 70% of business revenue, the second revenue stream has been expanding at a double-digit annual pace. In 2014, 60% of their customers visited for Total Car Care, and they expect that number to rise as they continue to advertise in national and local markets.

They calculate that the average automobile customer will spend more than $50,000 on repair during the time they own and operate a car. If that customer has two vehicles — and most households have two vehicles or more — that amount doubles. Even though the average transmission rebuild costs a customer about $2,500, total spending on transmission work is a small fraction of car care spending. Most people only consider replacing a transmission on a vehicle once. They get oil changes, brake work and tune-ups continually. The bulk of that $50,000-per-customer lifetime spending goes toward other repair services.

They believe that the real power and direction of the AAMCO franchise opportunity going forward is by leveraging expertise in transmissions into Total Car Care, and increasing the value of every customer — who will become lifetime customers instead of transactional ones, and they are able to grab an increasingly large share of those customers' car repair dollars.

AAMCO states that the total investment to open a new AAMCO auto franchise ranges from $227,400 to $333,000. This figure includes a $39,500 franchise fee, as well as the costs for equipment, training, leasing a property, and other items outlined in the chart below.

Franchise candidates should have a minimum of $65,000 in liquid capital and a net worth of at least $250,000 to get started. The decision to open an AAMCO franchise is a major investment, which is why we offer a number of financing options that make it possible for us to partner with the most passionate owners in the industry.

The following breakdown of start-up costs provided by AAMCO will give the reader a good example of the various start-up costs that would be required by many new ventures, whether a franchise operation or a stand-alone company providing a product or service.

A BUSINESS OF YOUR OWN

ESTIMATED INITIAL INVESTMENT

Initial License Fee	$39,500	Installments
Business Coach Training	$10,000	Lump Sum
AAMCO Security Deposit	$5,000	Lump Sum
Grand Opening Advertising Expenses	$3,000	Lump Sum
Travel Expenses for Training Program	$2,000 -$4,000	As incurred
Real Estate & Utility Deposits	$14,000 -$43,000	As incurred
Leasehold Improvements	$8,500 -$12,000	As arranged
Signs - 8	$7,500 -$19,000	As agreed
Shop Equipment, Supplies, Lifts &	$78,400 -$98,000	As agreed
POS System	$3,500	Lump Sum
Computers and Phone System-Hardware	$7,000 -$10,000	As incurred
Office Furniture	$6,000 -$7,000	As incurred
Sales Materials	$800 -$1,000	Lump Sum
Technical Information System	$1,700	Lump Sum
Technical Information System	$300	Installment
Other Costs & Professional Fees	$4,000 -$10,000	As incurred
Insurance	$1,500 -$2,500	As incurred
Advertising Costs (13 weeks)	$4,700 -$13,500	As agreed
Additional Funds	$30,000 -$50,000	As incurred

SUBWAY - Fred DeLuca and Peter Buck opened the first Subway in Bridgeport, Connecticut in August, 1965. Then, they set a goal of having thirty-two stores opened in ten years. Fred soon learned the basics of running a business, as well as the importance of serving a well-made, high quality product, providing excellent customer service, keeping operating costs low and finding great locations. These early lessons continue to serve as the foundation for successful SUBWAY® restaurants around the world.

By 1974 they owned sixteen submarine sandwich shops throughout Connecticut. They then decided to start franchising, launching the company into rapid growth which continues to this day.

They claim that today, the SUBWAY® brand is the world's largest submarine sandwich chain with more than 37,000 locations around the world. They claim to be the leading choice for people seeking quick, nutritious meals that the whole family can enjoy. As they continue to grow, they are guided by the passion for delighting customers by serving fresh, delicious, made-to-order sandwiches.

In the United States and Canada, the franchise fee is $15,000. In countries outside of North America the initial franchise fee ranges from $10,000 - $15,000 (USD).

The total investment is an estimated $116,000 to $263,000 in the United States and $102,000 to $234,000 in Canada.

SUBWAY® franchisees pay 12.5% every week (gross sales minus the sales tax); 8% goes toward the franchise royalties and 4.5% toward advertising.

All new franchisees attend a two-week training course at World Headquarters, or one of the many training centers around the world. Once training is complete, on-going support comes in many forms, including local development offices, e-learning training courses, a weekly newsletter and much more.

Taco Bell - Advantages cited by Taco Bell of being a Taco Bell franchisee:

- Access to nationally and internationally known products, as well as a proven operating system that sets the franchisee up to compete in multi-unit Mexican restaurant franchising.
- Strong brand awareness of the nation's leading Mexican-inspired franchise.
- A peer network of more than 350 franchisees, more than 35% of which have more than 25 years of experience.
- More than fifty years of Taco Bell multi-unit Mexican franchise support and many programs to help the franchisee compete within the franchise industries.
- Access to the United Foodservice Purchasing Cooperative (UFPC), the largest food-buying co-op in the foodservice industry.

Training and Support

Taco Bell believes that quality training and support are the foundation to building a multi-unit Mexican restaurant franchise business. The Taco Bell Mexican food franchise system, has four primary areas of emphasis:

1. Establishing key contacts
2. Building your restaurant
3. Building your team
4. Setting up a strong start for the restaurant franchise

Taco Bell provides training for franchisees and restaurant managers, including brand education as well as various levels of Mexican restaurant franchise training. Lasting six to eight weeks and consisting of web-based, on-the-job and classroom training, the program is taught by a certified Taco Bell training instructor in a certified Taco Bell training restaurant. This education should be completed at least six weeks prior to the planned opening of a Mexican food franchise.

Taco Bell believes that ongoing support is also necessary for the Mexican restaurant franchise, so they provide coaching, recognition and continuous backing for franchisees. This team also coordinates product and procedure rollouts regularly during the course of the year. Taco Bell corporate support includes:

- Recommendations on how to conduct a grand opening while being reimbursed up to $5,000 of documented expenses.
- An annual convention featuring a full-day of presentations from Taco Bell brand leadership, keynote addresses, and many choices for continuing professional education opportunities for the Mexican franchise.
- Regional association membership – meetings focus more closely on topics such as operations and team training.
- Regular town hall calls held by the Taco Bell Leadership Team to keep Taco Bell franchisees in the know with multi-unit restaurant franchise information while giving the opportunity to ask questions on important front line issues.

- A wide range of optional continuing education courses through Yum! University.
- For a traditional Taco Bell restaurant franchise unit, the total estimated investment ranges between $1,193,300 - 2,465,600, which includes the initial franchise fee of $45,000. For an end-cap Mexican food franchise unit, the total investment ranges from $585,300-$1,205,600, which includes the $25,000 initial franchise fee. The total investment to begin operation of an existing Taco Bell fast food franchise ranges between $175,000-$1,445,000 (or more), excluding real property.

Budget Car Rental - Budget Car Rental offers franchise opportunities to those who can demonstrate the ability to build and maintain a profitable business along with the support of a solid global brand. They invite exceptional entrepreneurs to join their successful international team as self-employed agency/independent operators by managing all operations of a Budget off-airport location.

As an independent operator, the franchisee is responsible for the growth and success of the Budget location. A major initial investment is not required. The franchisee is authorized to rent Budget's vehicles, staff the location, and control costs of the operation.

Start-up fees are generally between $5,000 and $10,000 and cover the costs of grand opening, supply inventory, organization expenses, insurance, uniforms, and computer equipment.

Independent operators are paid a commission on rental revenue. Budget offers the dedicated assistance of their experienced support staff in all phases of the operation.

Budget will provide the franchisee with an appropriate selection of late model rental cars to meet the projected demand.

While it is helpful to have experience in the operation of a business such as car rental, hotel, or other travel related business, it is not a requirement to become a Budget independent operator.

Key success criteria include:

- The ability to communicate effectively with customers and employees.

A BUSINESS OF YOUR OWN

- A positive, goal-oriented, personality and a willingness to do everything it takes to build the business on a community basis.
- An outgoing community focus that might include joining the Chamber of Commerce, sponsoring local sports teams, and encouraging local businesses to refer customers.
- The ability to effectively serve customers and build a strong, thriving business.

An independent operator has unlimited potential for growth within the initial location or by taking on additional locations that may become available.

CHAPTER **12**

Franchise Opportunities

THIS WILL GIVE you a range of the investments required for various industries.

- **Money Mizer Pawns & Jewelers Franchise -**
  Cash Required: $150,000   Industry: Retail Franchises
- **All Tune And Lube**
  Cash Required: $30,000   Industry: Automotive Franchises
- **Retro Fitness**
  Cash Required: $300,000   Industry: Health & Fitness
- **Mr. Rooter Corporation**
  Cash Required: $50,000   Industry: Home Related
- **Mr. Appliance**
  Cash Required: $50,000   Industry: Home Related
- **Allstate - Minnesota, Illinois, Wisconsin**
  Cash Required: $50,000   Industry: Financial Services
- **Ace Hardware Corporation**
  Cash Required: $250,000   Industry: Home Related
- **PuroClean**
  Cash Required: $75,000   Industry: Cleaning & Maintenance
- **Fantastic Sams**
  Cash Required: $50,000   Industry: Retail Franchises
- **Fresh Coat**
  Cash Required: $45,000   Industry: Home Related

A BUSINESS OF YOUR OWN

- **Diamond International**
  Cash Required: $24,750   Industry: Work From Home
- **American Business Systems**
  Cash Required: $19,990   Industry: Business Opportunities
- **Growth Coach**
  Cash Required: $45,000   Industry: Business Services
- **Maids International**
  Cash Required: $60,000   Industry: Home Related
- **Liberty Tax Service**
  Cash Required: $50,000   Industry: Business Services
- **Snap Fitness**
  Cash Required: $75,000   Industry: Health & Fitness
- **ServiceMaster Residential**
  Cash Required: $25,000   Industry: Cleaning & Maintenance
- **Maaco**
  Cash Required: $140,000   Industry: Auto Painting & Repair
- **Duraclean**
  Cash Required: $35,000   Industry: Cleaning Services
- **Dickey's Barbecue Pit**
  Cash Required: $100,000   Industry: Barbecue Restaurant
- **American Business Systems**
  Cash Required: $20,000   Industry: Medical Billing
- **The Tutoring Center**
  Cash Required: $40,000   Industry: Education
- **Steamatic**
  Cash Required: $75,000   Industry: Cleaning Services

CHAPTER 13

Franchise Ratings

Below is a list of the top 10 Franchises for 2015 listed by Entrepreneur.com

Rank	Franchise Name	Startup Cost
1	Hampton by Hilton	$4M - 14M
2	Anytime Fitness	$63K - 418K
3	Subway	$117K - 263K
4	Jack in the Box	$1M - 2M
5	Supercuts	$114K - 234K
6	Jimmy John's Gourmet Sandwiches	$323K - 544K
7	Servpro	$142K - 191K
8	Denny's Inc.	$1M - 2M
9	Pizza Hut Inc.	$297K - 2M
10	7-Eleven Inc.	$38K - 1M

A BUSINESS OF YOUR OWN

Below is a list of the top 100 Global Franchises - Rankings (2015) by Franchise Direct

Rank	Franchise Name	Industry
1	SUBWAY®	Sandwich & Bagel Franchises
2	McDonald's	Fast Food Franchises
3	KFC	Chicken Franchises
4	Burger King	Fast Food Franchises
5	7 Eleven	Convenience Store Franchises
6	Hertz	Car Rental & Dealer Franchises
7	Pizza Hut	Pizza Franchises
8	Ace Hardware Corporation	Home Improvement Retail Franchises
9	Wyndham Hotels and Resorts	Hotel Franchises
10	Groupe Casino	Food & Grocery Retail Franchises
11	GNC Live Well	Wellness Products & Services
12	RE/MAX	Real Estate Franchises
13	Carrefour	Convenience Store Franchises
14	Dunkin' Donuts	Bakery & Donut Franchises

FRANCHISE RATINGS

15	InterContinental Hotels and Resorts	Hotel Franchises
16	Hilton Hotels & Resorts	Hotel Franchises
17	Domino's Pizza	Pizza Franchises
18	Marriott International	Hotel Franchises
19	Taco Bell	Fast Food Franchises
20	DIA	Convenience Store Franchises
21	Baskin-Robbins	Ice Cream Franchises
22	Tim Hortons	Bakery & Donut Franchises
23	Choice Hotels	Hotel Franchises
24	Papa John's	Pizza Franchises
25	Snap-on Tools	Automotive Repair Franchises
26	JAN-PRO Cleaning Systems	Commercial Cleaning Franchises
27	Wendy's	Fast Food Franchises
28	Jani-King Commercial Cleaning Services	Commercial Cleaning Franchises
29	Circle K	Convenience Store Franchises
30	Europcar	Car Rental & Dealer Franchises
31	Century 21	Real Estate Franchises
32	Sign-A-Rama	Sign, Print & Copy Stores
33	Dairy Queen	Fast Food Franchises
34	NOVUS Glass	Auto Glass Franchises

35	Groupe Auchan	Food & Grocery Retail Franchises
36	Meineke Car Care Center	Automotive Repair Franchises
37	Kumon	Child Education Franchises
38	Snap Fitness	Gym Franchises
39	Midas	Automotive Repair Franchises
40	Chem-Dry Carpet Cleaning	Carpet Cleaning Franchises
41	No+Vello	Spa Franchises
42	Anytime Fitness Inc.	Gym Franchises
43	Popeyes Louisiana Kitchen	Fast Food Franchises
44	Ziebart	Car Detailing Franchises
45	ServiceMaster Clean	Commercial Cleaning Franchises
46	Auntie Anne's Pretzels	Bakery & Donut Franchises
47	Hardee's	Fast Food Franchises
48	H&R Block	Financial Services
49	Vanguard Cleaning Systems	Commercial Cleaning Franchises
50	Sylvan Learning	Children & Education
51	ActionCOACH	Business Consulting Services
52	Coldwell Banker Residential	Real Estate Franchises
53	Yogen Fruz	Frozen Yogurt Franchises
54	Yves Rocher	Cosmetic Franchises
55	EmbroidMe	Embroidery Businesses

FRANCHISE RATINGS

56	Coverall Health-Based Cleaning System®	Commercial Cleaning Franchises
57	Long John Silver's	Fast Food Franchises
58	Maaco Collision Repair & Auto Painting	Automotive Repair Franchises
59	Gold's Gym	Gym Franchises
60	Arby's	Burger Franchises
61	Liberty Tax Service	Tax Franchises
62	Cinnabon	Bakery & Donut Franchises
63	Denny's	Burger Franchises
64	Molly Maid	House Cleaning Franchises
65	The UPS Store	Mailing & Shipping Franchises
66	International House of Pancakes (IHOP)	Fast Food Franchises
67	Little Caesars	Pizza Franchises
68	Merry Maids	House Cleaning Franchises
69	Smoothie King	Smoothie Franchises
70	100 Montaditos	Restaurant Franchises
71	Matco Tools	Automotive Repair Franchises
72	Naturhouse	Wellness Products & Services
73	FASTSIGNS®	Printer, Copying & Sign Franchises
74	The Coffee Bean & Tea Leaf	Café Franchises
75	Edible Arrangements®	Gift Franchises

#	Name	Category
76	Minuteman Press	Printer, Copying & Sign Franchises
77	VOM FASS	Specialty Retail Franchises
78	Supercuts	Hair & Beauty Salon Franchises
79	MRI Network	Personnel Services
80	Tutor Doctor	Tutoring Franchises
81	Pita Pit	Fast Food Franchises
82	Cartridge World	Office Supplies Franchises
83	Husse	Pet Store Franchises
84	PIRTEK USA	Industrial Franchises
85	CruiseOne	Cruise Franchises
86	Express Employment Professionals	Employment & Staffing Franchises
87	5àSec	Clothing Franchises
88	Applebees	Burger Franchises
89	Cold Stone Creamery®	Ice Cream Franchises
90	Jiffy Lube®	Oil Change Franchises
91	Martinizing Dry Cleaning	Dry-cleaning Franchises
92	Sport Clips	Hair Salon Franchises
93	Mathnasium	Child Education Franchises
94	Furniture Medic	Repair & Painting Franchises
95	Precision Tune Auto Care	Automotive Repair Franchises
96	Ben & Jerry's Franchising, Inc.	Ice Cream Franchises

97	Johnny Rockets	Burger Franchises
98	Mr. Handyman	Handyman Franchises
99	A&W Restaurants	Restaurant Franchises
100	Great Clips	Hair Salon Franchises

CHAPTER **14**

Evaluating Franchise Opportunities

THERE ARE LITERALLY hundreds of franchise opportunities available for your consideration. The list just keeps growing. Virtually every industry which can be served by small enterprises offers franchise opportunities. The franchisors emphasize the lucrative advantages of the business plan they are offering in selling the opportunities to the franchisee. There are many franchise brokers who specialize in selling franchises. The brokers emphasize the lucrativeness of the business opportunities they represent. Although the emphasis of profitability of opportunities may be substantial, in order to make a rational decision about a given franchise opportunity you should do your own due diligence. You should determine the opportunity's suitability for your financial capability, the likelihood of success given your personal characteristics, your motivation for the industry, and willingness to meet the operational requirements.

Due Diligence - Questions worthy of consideration in selecting a franchise:

<u>Longevity</u> – How long has the franchisor been in business? Start-up franchises are sometimes successful but can be risky. If the product or service is not popular, not right for the given areas, or not

competitive, the franchisor can fail and take all of the franchisees down with them.

Financial Strength – Is the franchisor financially sound? What is the risk of the franchisor failing financially, seeking bankruptcy, or simply ceasing to do business? You want that risk to be as near zero as you can find it. Ask to review their financial strength. Ask your accountant to analyze their financial statements to assure their viability.

Success – How successful are the existing franchisees. What is the success rate, the failure rate? Interview as many existing franchisees as possible, not just those they offer for reference, but those you select on your own. Look for comments online about the franchisor. In some states there are requirements for franchisors to provide prospective franchisees a complete list of current franchisees for reference regarding the success of the franchise operation, prior to committing to an acquisition.

Cost of Franchise – The cost of the franchise should be considered as if one was acquiring an ongoing business or launching a new enterprise. The cost of the franchise, typically the franchise fee and other training and start-up costs, should be included along with the facility, equipment, inventory and working capital investments.

Profitability – What are the profit margins, operating profits, and net income? This must be considered after deducting the franchise fee as an expense. The ongoing franchise fee is a cost of business just like any other cost of sales. If the franchisor states that the product or service has a 50% profit margin on sales, you must consider the franchise fee a cost as well. Do your own math. The franchisor receives a percent of sales, but the franchisee pays all expenses including rent, payroll, cost-of-sales, insurance, and other operating expenses. The product or service should be capable of yielding a sale price adequate to cover the franchise fee and provide a normal bottom line income margin commensurate with financial standards for a non-franchised business.

Resale Policy – Investigate the resale policy of the franchisor. Can you sell your franchise to another? What are the terms? Must you pay a portion of the sale price to the franchisor? What are the selection requirements of the franchisor? What is your recourse for the franchisor's refusal of a buyer that seems qualified but is denied by the franchisor for the acquisition?

Product or Service – How unique is the product or service? Do you have an advantage over a competitor who lacks access to the product or service? Does the brand name exude a level of quality or reliability that is advantageous? Does the franchisor stay abreast of changing technology in the industry for the benefit of the franchisees? Do they upgrade their products or service to be an industry leader?

Diversification Policy – Does the franchise agreement prohibit the franchisee from participating in other businesses or acquiring additional franchised locations within the same franchise? Is there a restriction on diversifying the product or service line to accommodate customer needs that the franchisor does not provide?

Training and Consultation – Does the franchisor provide adequate training and ongoing consultation for the benefit of the franchisee?

Sale of Franchisor – Does the franchisor have the right to sell the parent company and leave all of the franchisees in place? Do the franchisees have any right of approval or denial of a sale of the franchisor? What is your recourse if the franchise company is sold to another owner who fails to honor the rights of franchisees? Would the cost of litigating such a dispute resolution be prohibitive for the franchisee?

Dispute Resolution – Is there a policy for resolution of a dispute between the franchisor and the franchisee? Is the policy advantageous for the franchisor? Would the cost of resolution representation or litigation be prohibitive for the franchisee?

Franchise Termination Policy – What are the terms of termination of the franchise agreement by franchisor for cause or lack of cause? Can you be terminated by franchisor? What is your recourse? Is there a restriction of due process? Can you demand a court hearing? Can you demand a jury trial? Is arbitration required? Is mediation required? Who selects arbitrators or mediators?

EVALUATING FRANCHISE OPPORTUNITIES

In order to fully evaluate the purchase of a franchise, all of the above suggestions should be considered. If the overall terms are questionable and not clearly acceptable, one may be better off selecting another opportunity or buying or launching a business without commitments that may end up to the disadvantage of the buyer.

CHAPTER **15**

Growing and Expanding Your Business

ONE OF THE best statements often quoted to business owners is simple but profound: If you have something to sell, don't keep it a secret. When it comes to growing your business, promotional marketing and advertising is tantamount. It can be expensive and time-consuming. It can be simple or it can require expertise. But it must be done. Not many businesses grow on word-of-mouth, upon which some business owners try to rely. You can't drive by a car dealership, a hotel or motel, an auto-service station, a car repair shop, a convenience store, a fast-food restaurant, a tax preparation office, real estate for sale or rent, a retail store, or a shopping center without seeing their sign inviting you to stop in and shop or use their services. You can't watch a TV show on network stations without seeing more commercials than you wish to endure. The evidence is everywhere. You just can't keep it a secret if you want to survive, and you can't survive if you don't build your business volume and continue to grow.

If you are starting a new business or if you are acquiring an existing business, you should always budget for marketing and advertising. If the business has an existing customer base, it will likely not stay that way unless you are continually reaching out for new business. Customers typically come and go. They go through attrition: no longer needing the service, going out of business, becoming disgruntled for some reason, a competitor offers better terms or more efficient service, new technology, and other reasons beyond your control. In order to retain your customer level you must bring on new customers. If you want to grow your business you must promote for even more new customers or offer even more new services beyond the point of offsetting the natural effects of customer loss through attrition.

There are various ways to grow your business:

New customers

Attraction of new customers is one of the least financially demanding ways of growing your company. With a concentrated sales effort and the right offering to potential customers, growth can be steady. Steady growth makes servicing the customer in a professional manner more easily fulfilled, and the additional effort required of your employees more easily accomplished.

Companies that grow steadily typically maintain a sales staff responsible for maintaining customer satisfaction, customer loyalty, and the ongoing addition of new customers. This function is often the primary responsibility of the company owner since nothing can be more important than maintaining and growing the customer base.

New products or services

Launching new products or services is a leading method of expansion for many companies. This may not require additional capital if the new products or services are compatible in design and performance to the existing lines. With expansion into new lines of products, such as those requiring new technologies, equipment, or processes, or expansion into new services which require additional personnel, special knowledge of personnel, and new training or qualification, the costs could be extraordinary and may require additional funding in order to provide the service in a timely and professional manner.

The most important aspects of offering new products or services would be: the assurance of customer demand, the company's ability to meet the demand, the company's ability to obtain any capital requirements for fulfilling the demand, and the profitability of the new product or service while meeting the pricing by competitors. Launching a new product or service should not be undertaken unless these essential aspects are reasonably certain.

New locations

Launching new locations can provide new business which cannot be competitively serviced from the existing location, either from the standpoint of customer contact, efficient delivery, or cost of servicing. The cost of establishing a new location could include additional physical facilities, additional personnel, compliance with regulations, or compliance with zoning restrictions. A prudent decision to expand in this way should include an exhaustive study of potential new business, the total cost of the expansion, and reasonable certainty of an adequate return on the required effort and investment.

Acquire competitors

Expansion by acquiring competitors seems to be the most often chosen and most lucrative means of expansion by many of the large corporations. Although acquisitions require capital or financing, this method of expansion is often the most efficient and most expedient in achieving growth. This process is what drives the mergers and acquisitions industry and the private equity groups of today. Many small companies have become larger by acquiring competitors. Many bigger companies have become much bigger by acquiring competitors. Big companies have become behemoths by acquiring or merging with competitors. The advantage is beyond the benefit of additional business and the profits therefrom. Often, the synergies and strategies of combining facilities, staff, and sales and marketing activities provide greater rewards than simply the profit from additional business. The mergers and acquisitions industry has evolved from a simple joining of two companies for expansion, to a huge industry in itself, creating large investment groups whose sole purpose is seeking merger candidates to join together, either to retain and operate, or to expand and resell for a substantial profit.

Consolidation of companies has created many behemoth corporations in the last 50 years, sometimes resulting in unpopular and devastating effects, such as: squeezing many smaller companies out of business, enabling profit margin enhancement by elimination of competition, establishing monopolistic enterprises, increasing executive compensation, exacerbating income inequality for workers, and establishing a feeling of insecurity for middle managers and the mass of lower income workers.

The results can be beneficial for investors. They can be devastating for those adversely effected. However, this remains the fastest and often the safest method of rapid growth for companies with capital made available by those seeking more lucrative investment opportunities, such as those made appealing by the history of successful outcomes of industry consolidations.

Merge with Competitors

Acquiring competitors may have insurmountable funding challenges due to size comparisons and financial resources. Merging with competitors may be a more feasible growth strategy, especially for smaller companies and those that are undercapitalized, and thus is more often accomplished. Merging two or more small companies often creates a more marketable size, a more reliable supplier, a stronger financial statement, a more diverse management structure, and a more stable work force. Funding for growth would generally be more attainable, both from the standpoint of financial stability and management stability. It could also be more attractive to a lender or investor.

Merging requires a great deal of desire on the part of the companies considering a merger. The challenges can involve leadership positions, ownership percentages, profit distribution, management compensation, dispute resolution, dissolution provisions, and many others. The most important consideration should be compatibility of the merging parties and the willingness to resolve disputes and reach consensus on operational and strategic issues.

There is always strength in size. Small companies are often considered fragile and risk-prone, making growth capital more difficult to attain. Larger enterprises are more desirable when selecting product or service suppliers, more attractive to lenders or investors, more sustainable financially, more desirable for employment in terms of income and advancement opportunities, and more sought-after as an acquisition candidate in any potential future sale or merger.

Business Consultants

Business consultants can be beneficial for small companies for preparation of growth plans, managerial advice, and development and implementation of finance. Business consultants should be selected based upon their experience and reputation in the particular industry in which they operate and their area of expertise. Some business consultants specialize in specific segments of business operations, such as: financial management, internet technology, business structure, staffing, advertising, promotion, sales management, mergers and acquisitions, or specific technological areas. Care should be taken in selecting a consultant proficient in the area of need for the specific objective, be it business operations, financing, promotion, acquisition for expansion, or sale of the enterprise.

Expansion Funding

Expansion funding sources depend to a large extent upon the size of the enterprise. There are many lending institutions around the country that do business acquisition lending, franchise lending, retail business lending, SBA lending, equipment purchase lending, and working capital lending, which is generally referred to as a bank line of credit.

If your company is small and without good bank collateral, such

GROWING AND EXPANDING YOUR BUSINESS

as equity in real estate, machinery and equipment, or other liquid assets, a bank loan is not an easy option. Bankers are not really in the risk business with small scale borrowers. Without good bank collateral, bank borrowing can often be accomplished through a Small Business Administration ("SBA") guarantee, which assures the bank of a percentage of repayment in the event of borrower default. Some financial institutions specialize in SBA loans. Some are granted SBIC, Small Business Investment Company status, whereby the financial institution can grant the loan without prior SBA approval.

The borrower should be aware that with SBA involvement in lending, the requirements are not lenient in terms of collateral or in terms of repayment. The SBA is required to take a lien on any collateral that you may have available. If you have not been in business for a number of years with acceptable profitability, approval is often difficult or unlikely, except for limited startup funds for some qualifying applicants.

SBA participates in a number of loan programs designed for business owners who may have trouble qualifying for a traditional bank loan.

To start the process, you should visit a local bank or lending institution that participates in SBA programs. SBA loan applications are structured to meet SBA requirements, so that the loan is eligible for an SBA guarantee. This guarantee represents the portion of the loan that SBA will repay to the lender if you default on your loan payments.

SBA - Starting and Expanding Businesses

- Basic 7(a) Loan Program
    Gives 7(a) loans to eligible borrowers for starting, acquiring and expanding a small business. This type of loan is the most basic and the most used within SBA's business loan programs. Borrowers must apply through a participating lender institution.
- Certified Development Company (CDC) 504 Loan Program
    Provides growing businesses with long-term, fixed-rate financing for major fixed assets, such as land and buildings.

- Microloan Program

    Offers very small loans to start-up, newly established or growing small business concerns. SBA makes funds available to nonprofit community-based lenders which, in turn, make loans to eligible borrowers in amounts up to a maximum of $50,000. Applications are submitted to the local intermediary and all credit decisions are made on the local level.

Disaster Loans

- Disaster Assistance Loans

    Provide financial assistance to victims of disasters or to individuals in a declared disaster area. You may be eligible for this type of loan even if you don't own a business.

- Economic Injury Loans

    Assist small businesses, small agricultural cooperatives and nonprofit organizations as they recover from economic losses resulting from physical disaster or an agricultural production disaster.

Export Assistance Loans

- Export Express

    Provide exporters and lenders with a streamlined method of obtaining financing for loans and lines of credit up to $500,000. Lenders use their own credit decision process and loan documentation; exporters get access to their funds faster. SBA provides an expedited eligibility review with a response in less than 24 hours.

- Export Working Capital

    Offers loans targeted at businesses that are able to generate export sales but need additional working capital to support these opportunities.

- International Trade Loans

    Gives term loans that are designed for businesses that plan to start/continue exporting or those that that have been

GROWING AND EXPANDING YOUR BUSINESS

adversely affected by competition from imports. The proceeds of the loan must enable the borrower to be in a better position to compete.

Veteran and Military Community Loans
- Military Reservist Economic Injury Disaster Loan
  Offers funds to eligible small businesses to meet ordinary and necessary operating expenses that could have been met, but are unable to meet, because an essential employee was "called-up" to active duty in their role as a military reservist.

Special Purpose Loans
- CAP Lines
  Help small businesses meet their short-term and cyclical working-capital needs through the SBA umbrella program called CAPLines.
- Pollution Control Loans
  Provides financing to eligible small businesses for the planning, design or installation of a pollution control facility.
- U.S. Community Adjustment and Investment Program (CAIP)
  CAIP is a program established to assist U.S. companies that are doing business in areas of the country that have been negatively affected by the North American Free Trade Agreement (**NAFTA**). To be eligible, a business must reside in a county noted as being negatively affected by NAFTA, based on job losses and the unemployment rate of the county.

As you can see from the above list of loan programs, the SBA offers financial assistance for various types of capital needs. The company applying for these programs should have good financial records and be capable of demonstrating that the borrowing company is viable and would have a good chance of sustainability once the financial assistance is approved.

CHAPTER 16

Private Equity Groups

PRIVATE EQUITY GROUPS are considered an attractive source for growth capital or a future sale of the company for many small to midsize business owners. However, they are not a financing alternative or growth funding source for most small business start-ups or acquisitions. They can be a source of funding for substantial growth or a future sale of the company if profitability and growth potential provide an opportunity for the group to build the company to a viable size for a future sale or merger. This can provide a beneficial outcome for the business owner.

Private Equity Groups ("PEGs") are groups of investors that attract funds from institutions, such as: pension funds, university endowment funds, hedge funds, or private investors, seeking a greater return on investment than what can be realized from bank interest or government bonds, which are typical risk-free investments. PEGs don't typically loan money to companies. They prefer to buy the company and operate it or do a joint venture with the owner by assuming a substantial ownership position and providing funds for growth and expansion. Their typical investment plan is to acquire the company or a portion of it, and increase income substantially to build the value for resale in a few years.

PEGs generally are not interested in small companies realizing less than a few million dollars of earnings. The investment in small companies is generally insufficient to satisfy the investment capital committed to them to invest for the institutions they represent.

A couple of decades ago there were a few private equity groups attracted to lower end middle market companies. The success they have generated from private equity investments, along with the lack of other attractive investment opportunities for institutional investors, has enabled this industry to create hundreds of such private equity groups around the globe.

PEGs generally seek companies with Earnings before Interest Taxes and Depreciation (EBITDA) of two million dollars or more. The larger PEGs require even larger earnings to induce their involvement. After acquiring a company or taking an ownership position, they invest capital for expansion, bring on additional advisors and managers to build the revenue and earnings, seek add-on acquisitions of companies in the same specific industry, and then resell the company, realizing a gain for the PEG and the institutional investor that provided the original funding.

PEGs generally have specific industries in which they pursue investment, industries in which they have come to have special knowledge or success, or industries that they consider good growth candidates.

Many PEGs prefer to acquire companies in which the owner is willing to stay on and run the company, along with their financial and managerial assistance. This plan often works out well for the seller who can retain a viable income and participate in the value enhancement going forward created by the PEG.

Private Equity Groups Investment Criteria

Below are some examples of inquiries from private equity groups that are seeking acquisitions. These inquiries illustrate the types of companies that are attractive to such investors and the various criteria of their focus. By reviewing the business features, criteria, and terms suggested, one can gain an understanding of the essential qualities of successful companies for long-term sustainability and growth potential – those qualities that entice the merger and acquisition community and provide rewarding exit strategies for business owners.

Permission to publish the names of various groups has not been obtained for this section, so the criteria, investment, and terms of engagement are listed without naming the company involved.

Group 1:

Investment Criteria
- At least $500,000 in free cash flow
- Minimum of 10% cash flow margins (EBITDA less cap ex)

Investment Size
- $2,000,000 – $10,000,000

Growth Expectations
- $5,000,000 in free cash flow in 3-7 years

Geography
- United States

Targeted Industries
- Business Services
- Distribution
- Financial Services
- Healthcare Services
- Information Services
- Niche Manufacturing
- Technology-enabled, Scalable businesses

Non-Targeted Industries
- Capital Intensive
- Consumer Products
- Real Estate
- Retail

Group 2:

Our exclusive focus is on management-led leveraged buyouts and recapitalizations of smaller lower-middle-market companies.

- We partner with management teams to acquire and help build small niche leaders, profitable, growth-ready businesses with revenues typically between $10 million and $75 million and EBITDA up to $8 million (add-on acquisitions for current platform companies typically generate at least $2 million in revenues).
- We typically invest $2 million to $30 million in management-led leveraged acquisitions, and make follow-on investments to support the internal growth and health of our portfolio companies.
- We are an opportunity-driven buyer; our portfolio includes companies in widely diverse niche manufacturing, distribution and specialty service markets.
- We are long-term investors. We focus on building companies over time and are committed to maximizing their values.
- We seek companies that fit these criteria:
  » Small and growth-ready;
  » A niche market;
  » A strong and defensible market position;
  » Consumer, commercial, manufacturing, distribution, services
  » Located in the United States.
  » Owners seeking retirement
  » Owners seeking capital for expansion

Group 3:

- **Investment Size -** Our ideal investment size range is $15 - $40 million. This transaction size allows us to often avoid the more competitive auction environment typically found in larger transactions. We expect to be the lead investor in transactions and often bring in limited partners as strategic co-investors in investment opportunities that require additional equity capital where our collective skills and experience can create value.

- **Stage of Development** - We seek to acquire cash flow positive companies in buyout transactions. The typical financial profile includes minimum revenue of $10.0 million and minimum EBITDA of $3.0 million.
- **Diversification** - We will not allocate more than 20% of the fund's capital to any single investment. Sector diversification within the targeted industry segments is also considered as we allocate our fund's capital.
- **Geography** - Our investment focus will be exclusively focused on businesses headquartered in North America. However, certain of our investment companies have international operations, sales and team members.
- **Investment Horizon** - We expect to realize investment returns through a sale, recapitalization or initial public offering within a three- to seven-year time frame. Investments that provide multiple exit strategies are preferred, but the key factor is finding companies to invest in that have superior growth profiles with dynamic, experienced executive teams.

Group 4:

We are a private equity group that makes control investments in high-quality, lower-middle market companies that have shown a consistent track record of success. For companies that have reached a performance level that finds them transitioning beyond being an entrepreneurial business, our firm can deliver the planning, experience, resources and capital to overcome critical constraints and build long-term value. With our disciplined approach, we work on minimizing the uncontrollable and turning previously chaotic scenarios into predictable business models.

We are actively looking for platform companies and add-on opportunities for several portfolio companies.

Group 5:

Our ideal target is a niche business that has strong growth potential, recurring or a repeat revenue base, and a focus on services. We avoid businesses that have a retail and heavy manufacturing focus.

Below are the characteristics of the business that we are seeking:

- Annual revenue of $5 million to $40 million
- Minimum cash flow of $750,000
- EBITDA margin of 10%+
- Owner seeking to exit in 0-3 years
- Demonstrated business or industry growth
- Owners and senior management are looking to step away from day-to-day operational control

Group 6:

Our investment criteria:

- Company located within 50-mile radius of following cities:
  » Seattle / Portland / San Francisco / L.A. / San Diego / Las Vegas / Phoenix
  » Boston / NYC / Philadelphia / Washington DC / Raleigh
  » Chicago / Denver / Dallas / Austin
- Owner operator seeking exit and liquidity
- $0.5M to $5M EBITDA
- 10%+ EBITDA margin
- History of positive and recurring cash flows
- Low to moderate customer concentration

We offer business owners an attractive exit opportunity, both to achieve financial liquidity and to transition out of daily operations. We have direct access to capital and seasoned entrepreneurs, investors and deal professionals. We can close quickly and bring significant growth capital and expertise.

Group 7:

We are a dedicated growth capital investment company, a leading global private equity investment firm with $19 billion equity capital under management. We seek to make both majority and minority investments in strong, growth-oriented businesses located throughout North America, South America and Europe. We will invest $5 million to $30 million in equity in a given company and target investments in profitable growth-oriented businesses with between $10 million and $100 million in revenues. We consider investments across all industries, but focus on certain high-growth sectors where we have extensive in-house expertise such as technology, healthcare, internet and media, consumer products and technology-enabled financial and business services.

Group 8:

This investment group is interested in acquisition targets as described below:

> Distributors of industrial products based in the Midwestern or Eastern United States
> Revenues between $30MM and $120MM
> EBITDA of over $3MM
> The company should have some value-added services such as:
>
> - Supply chain solutions (for example, dispensing and vendor management inventory)
> - Repair and remanufacturing
> - Field service
> - Technical expertise
>
> President/CEO position may be vacated if desired

Group 9:

We specialize in helping business owners transition out of their business. We have a track record of working with owners to facilitate and quickly close transactions that meet their needs while ensuring that employees, customers and vendors are well taken care of throughout the transition.

Our investment criteria:

- Financial: $750k - $5M EBITDA
- Situational: Need for day to day management

We focus on businesses with EBITDA between $750k to $5M that are in need of management and capital. We are industry and geographically agnostic. The two most common situations include: retirement and rapidly growing businesses that may have outgrown the current ownership/management.

Group 10:

Our investment criteria:

Type Business:	Technology based manufacturing or value-added distribution businesses. Material science or performance material business with proprietary products preferred.
Markets:	Businesses that serve the electronic materials, telecommunications, personal care, energy, pharmaceutical or semiconductor markets.
Sales Volume:	$5,000,000 to $15,000,000
EBITDA:	$500,000 or greater
Geography:	Will consider opportunities nationwide, with preference to Midwest, Southeast or West Coast. We are a merchant-banking firm that provides buy-side representation to private-equity groups, corporations and industry-specific management teams in the middle market.

CHAPTER 17

Operating Financial Models

THE FOLLOWING EXAMPLES of financial profiles of various businesses can be helpful in understanding the features of sound financial management and the pitfalls that can lead to failure. Attention is given to various financial features, such as: capital requirements, asset requirements, liability prudence, income, expenses, profit margins, and tolerance of income interruptions or adverse economic occurrences. These examples can provide a basis of understanding when considering the acquisition of an existing company, projecting pro forma income for a start-up company, considering the financial health of your company as a going concern, or initiating reorganizational or operating decisions to enhance revenue and profitability.

The following is the Profit / (Loss) Statement of a small franchised ice cream shop in California.

First section - Sales, Cost of Goods Sold and Gross Profit.

Ice Cream Shop Profit/(Loss)			
	2007	2008	2009
Sales	202,911	241,619	182,355
Cost of Goods Sold:	(34,348)	(41,793)	(32,456)
Gross Profit	168,563	199,826	149,899

The next section shows an itemization of operating expenses, which, after deducting them from gross profit, gives us net income from operations.

OPERATING FINANCIAL MODELS

Expenses:			
Advertising & Promotion	1,291	5,421	420
Amortization	1,030	5,116	
Auto Expense	1,049	7,806	5,249
Bank Charges	350	2,897	1,969
Contributions	410	2,070	
Depreciation	7,758	46,223	9,455
Insurance- Liability	2,819	9,303	3,154
Insurance-Health	2,024	4,862	2,000
Interest	3,400	22,611	3,265
Laundry & Uniforms	700	681	344
Licenses & Permits	1,191	2,100	1,611
Miscellaneous	92	343	542
Office Supplies	318	1,240	1,724
Outside Services	270	764	227
Payroll	18,017	28,759	8,866
Payroll taxes	2,105	3,296	1,091
Professional Fees	750	3,093	675
Rent	11,061	34,300	25,195
Repairs & Maintenance	126	2,336	308
Royalties	8,567	12,542	
Security	565	997	
Supplies	5,176	19,094	
Telephone & Internet	1,987	3,966	2,039
Travel & Entertainment		534	329
Utilities	1,690	10,294	4,120
Total Expenses	74,746	230,648	72,583
Net Operating Income	**93,817**	**(30,822)**	**77,316**

From net income from operations we make adjustments to arrive at discretionary earnings.

Adjustments			
Amortization	1,030	5,116	
Contributions	2,410	2,070	
Depreciation	7,758	6,223	9,455
Interest	3,400	22,611	3,265
Personal Auto Use	500	3,900	2,600
Total Adjustments	15,098	79,920	15,320
Discretionary Earnings	**108,915**	**49,098**	**92,636**

Adjustments explained:

Depreciation deductions are not cash expenses during the years reported but were cash payments in the past when the depreciating assets were purchased. They are included as expenses for tax deduction purposes while the undepreciated portion of the original cost of the assets remains on the books. Depreciation is added back to earnings in this analysis since it is not a cash payment in the current year.

Amortization is not a cash expense during the years reported and is added back to earnings for the current year. It represents the payment for the initial organizational costs, acquired goodwill or other intangible assets, and is deducted from current income for tax purposes.

Interest is not an operating expense. It is a cost of capital, which would vary depending upon the capitalization of the current ownership and should not be considered an operating expense in the determination of operating income. Interest is added back to earnings for the current year.

Contributions and personal auto use are not operating expenses and should be considered non-business expenditures or perquisites of the company owners and are therefore added back to earnings for the current year.

This comparison of operating income reflects some important considerations in evaluating the financial health of the company. Some questions that should require additional review would include:

1. Note that the profit margin remains consistent through the three years at 80% or above. This is an accounting decision to include only merchandise purchases in cost of sales, and not to include the cost of labor and supplies. One might want to consider these expenses when determining the adequacy of profit margins to cover operating expenses and profit.
2. The revenue dropped significantly in 2009. Was that due to economic conditions, ownership distraction, declining geographic area, or other reasons? Will this trend correct or continue?
3. The discretionary earnings actually increased on lower sales in 2009. However, royalties were not paid to the parent company and no supplies were purchased, Security was eliminated, and payroll was substantially reduced. Was the payroll reduced due to shorter hours, increased owner hours worked, or declining sales? If the owners worked additional hours, the statement should be adjusted to reflect a normal payroll cost for the difference. What would have been the earnings if these items: royalties, security, and payroll, were normalized comparably with prior years?
4. How can revenue be increased to assure a financially healthy level? Could it be increased through improvement in economic conditions, advertising, ownership diligence, staffing changes, new products, or other factors?

The following P&L Statement reflects the earnings of a manufacturer of ventilation equipment for manufacturing applications, big-box retailers such as supermarkets, and general product retailers.

Ventilation Equipment Mfg Co.
P&L Comparisons
Periods - 2003 - 2004

	2003	2004
Total Sales	14,553,056	14,053,364
Cost of Goods Sold	8,163,713	8,184,459
Gross Profit	6,389,343	5,868,905
Selling Expenses	1,977,033	1,901,520
General & Administrative Expenses	2,763,693	2,624,084
Operating Income (Loss)	1,648,617	1,343,301
Other Income (Expense)	54,331	96,201
Net Income (Loss)	1,702,948	1,439,502
Adjustments:		
Amortization	82,054	82,054
Depreciation	95,063	66,222
Officer salary adjust to market	250,000	250,000
Other Income	(54,331)	(96,201)
Total Adjustments	481,448	302,075
EBITDA	2,184,396	1,741,577

This company has been in business for many years. They are a leader in their particular product line as a recognizable brand name. They are financially healthy, stable and debt free. Although they are on the smaller end of the financial scale preferred for private equity group investments, they can be leveraged up with new debt to fund new acquisitions for growth and to provide up-front management fees to attract private equity group principals. These factors increase the value of such a company beyond a normal low multiple of earnings valuation for smaller and more fragile companies.

The company reflects gross profit margins greater than 40%, sales expenses greater than 10%, net income greater than 10%, and EBITDA greater than 10%. All of these factors indicate a financially healthy company which continues to promote business aggressively, manages debt prudently, and maintains current industry technology.

OPERATING FINANCIAL MODELS

The following P&L Statement represents the earnings of a jewelry manufacturing company which manufactures a complete line of fine quality gold and silver jewelry:

Jewelry Manufacturing Co. P&L Comparisons 2002 - 2004			
	2002	2003	2004
Sales	8,749,051	10,003,293	8,649,606
Cost of Goods Sold	7,378,661	8,706,518	7,685,613
Gross Profit	1,370,390	1,296,775	963,993
Profit Margin	16%	13%	11%

This company manufactures jewelry from raw materials such as gold, silver and other materials. Note that the profit margins on sales are somewhat low, particularly for a manufacturer in a market of fluctuating values of precious metals. Low profit margins make it difficult to realize a profit after operating expenses are included.

A BUSINESS OF YOUR OWN

Expenses			
Advertising	49,940	37,747	40,188
Amortization	177,869	151,959	139,238
Automobile	10,094	6,157	8,572
Bad Debts	103,070		
Bank Charges	15,167	37,114	17,730
Charitable Contributions	2,148	1,100	
Commission	5,332	13,102	42,192
Depreciation	37,871	60,774	29,629
Dues & Subscriptions	4,862	5,367	6,506
Equipment Rental	24,694	19,582	10,773
Insurance	41,581	48,633	54,936
Insurance-Work Comp.	5,355	11,359	
Interest Expense	238,036	258,754	284,233
Legal & Professional	49,312	25,675	68,619
Office Expense	27,105	10,505	18,624
Postage	9,504	13,066	21,721
Rent	48,000	48,000	51,200
Repairs & Maintenance	12,873	10,679	9,307
Salaries & Wages	254,484	290,091	246,427
Salaries-Officers	73,360	73,360	73,360
Security	10,355	5,121	4,719
Supplies	27,492	16,336	
Taxes & Licenses	62,298	71,597	76,217
Telephone	17,340	17,315	18,055
Trade Shows, Promotion	24,296		
Travel & Entertainment	13,755	20,665	13,108
Utilities	23,302	20,936	21,713
Total Expenses	**1,369,495**	**1,274,994**	**1,257,067**

In the above section, note that operating expenses are equivalent to or greater than profit margins, yielding a breakeven or loss of income from operations.

Net Income Before Taxes	895	21,781	(293,074)
Adjustments:			
Amortization	177,869	151,959	139,238
Depreciation	136,983	218,708	110,962
Interest Expense	238,036	258,754	284,233
Officer Salary adjust to market	(150,000)	(150,000)	(150,000)
Total Adjustments	402,888	479,421	384,433
EBITDA	**403,783**	**501,202**	**91,359**

OPERATING FINANCIAL MODELS

This jewelry company competes with major manufacturers that have distribution channels through chains of retail stores. Most rely upon several large clients and many small retailers and wholesalers of their products.

The company, in order to finance operations, utilizes a gold leasing program offered by companies providing financing for the jewelry manufacturing industry. If the price of gold fluctuates, the company is faced with fluctuating costs of interest on the gold in their inventory. This factor adversely affects their cost of goods when the gold price rises and thus impacts their profit margin. The margin reflected in this P&L indicates above normal cost of goods and hence questionable financial stability of the company.

A more aggressive sales effort, with an inside-the-industry sales force, may provide greater sales and possibly greater profit margins. However, without improved margins the company probably would have limited value, other than possible merger with or liquidation to an industry competitor who may be able to profit from synergies of added customer base, additional manufacturing capacity, or technological improvements.

Business Acquisition / Disposition Sanity Test

The following is a comparison of various structures of an acquisition or disposition that could be considered in a sanity test format. A buyer of a business could use a sanity test such as this in determining the prudence of an acquisition. A seller of a business could use a sanity test such as this in determining the likelihood of finding a prudent buyer at a transaction price that meets the seller's objectives.

Pro Forma Cash Flow of a Subject Company

The subject business has average annual gross revenue of $750,000 for several years. The company has seller's discretionary earnings of $150,000. This, of course, includes net income before taxes, owner's salary, and any perquisites and benefits the owner receives. The sale price for the business is $250,000. The working capital the buyer must provide is estimated at $80,000.

Based upon this, the seller will pay all liabilities and retain the cash and cash equivalent assets. This amounts to $70,000. There is $30,000 in accounts payable and no bank debt or other liabilities. So, under this scenario the owner would receive a total net amount of $290,000 ($250,000+$70,000-$30,000), less any escrow fees or broker fees.

The buyer could be looking at various acquisition financing scenarios:

Business Acquisition – Sanity Test	
Acquisition Cost	$250,000
Down Payment – 20%	50,000
Working Capital Required	80,000
Financing Required	200,000
Terms: 10 years @ 7.5%	
Total Cash Investment	$130,000
Gross Sales of the Company	$750,000
Projected Operating Profit	150,000
Acquisition Financing Debt Service	(30,000)
Annual Improvements Required	(10,000)
Expected Return on Cash Investment-10%	(13,000)
Balance - Owner's Discretionary Earnings	$97,000

Business Acquisition – Sanity Test	
Acquisition Cost	$250,000
Down Payment – 100%	250,000
Working Capital Required	80,000
Total Cash Investment	$330,000
Gross Sales of the Company	$750,000
Projected Operating Profit	150,000
Acquisition Financing Debt Service	
Annual Improvements Required	(10,000)
Expected Return on Cash Investment-10%	(33,000)
Balance - Owner's Discretionary Earnings	$107,000

OPERATING FINANCIAL MODELS

Business Acquisition – Sanity Test	
Acquisition Cost	$250,000
Down Payment – 40%	100,000
Working Capital Required	80,000
Financing Required	150,000
Terms: 10 years @ 7.5%	
Total Cash Investment	**180,000**
Gross Sales of the Company	$750,000
Projected Operating Profit	150,000
Acquisition Financing Debt Service	(22,000)
Annual Improvements Required	(10,000)
Expected Return on Cash Investment-10%	(18,000)
Balance - Owner's Discretionary Earnings	**$100,000**

In analyzing the sanity of this acquisition we should consider some questions:

- What is the risk of failure?
- Can the business be expanded?
- Are the annual earnings sufficient for the buyer?
- Is the debt non-recourse or guaranteed by the buyer?
- Would seller financing be better for the buyer?
- Would seller financing be better for the seller?
- Does the future of the industry look promising?
- Is the return on invested cash sufficient for the risk?
- Are the buyer's earnings sufficient after deducting a typical salary for the owner working there full-time?

Questions such as these can be important considerations in acquisition negotiations and in agreeing on the value of a business enterprise. They can support a buyer's decision to buy or they can convince the buyer to decline. They can support the seller's decision to proceed or they can convince the seller to retain the company. A meeting of the objectives of both parties should be met in order to structure a prudent acquisition and sale of a company.

A Case of Accounting Irregularities

A business advisor was engaged by the owner of a company selling and installing car stereos, custom wheels and other auto accessories. The owner's proclaimed desire was to return to his country of origin outside the U.S.

The advisor reviewed the financial statements provided by the owner.

	2010	2011
Sales	$1,320,489	$1,315,002
Cost of Goods Sold:		
Beginning Inventory	215,000	772,007
Purchases	604,588	573,396
Ending Inventory	(386,538)	(714,262)
Total Cost of Goods	443,050	631,141
Gross Profit	877,439	683,861
Operating Expenses	575,753	381,640
Net Income	301,686	302,221

Sales were level over a two year period at $1.3 million. Costs of goods sold were $443,000 and $631,000 respectively. Gross profits were $877,000 and $683,000 respectively. Operating expenses were $575,753 and $381,640 respectively. Net income was level at $302,000.

From a quick glance, this may look all well and good. The financial statement reflected gross profit margins of 67% and 53%, very healthy profit margins (maybe "too good to be true"). It reflected net income margins of 23%, very healthy bottom lines. Most companies could only strive for such levels of financial performance.

However, looking in more detail, the beginning inventory in the first year was $215,000 and the ending inventory was $386,000, no problem there. But the beginning inventory in the second year was $772,000 - impossible. You can't have an increase in inventory from one day to the next of 100% without it being reflected in purchases or adjustments. This discrepancy is an obvious "red flag." If such a situation had occurred it would have necessitated adjustments that are not reflected in the statements provided.

OPERATING FINANCIAL MODELS

Another abnormality which would require some scrutiny and explanation is that the net income was level but the gross profit margins were off by $180,000. Not a normal situation.

The store was open seven days per week, from 9:00 a.m. until 9:00 p.m. That is 360 hours per month. They employed a manager, a stock employee, one or more floor salespeople at all times, one or more service employees at all times. At a minimum, that adds up to four employees to seven at all times or more at busy times. If you use five as the minimum number, the hours per month would be 1,800. The payroll at minimum wage plus payroll taxes and work comp insurance would be $225,000. If we use six employees as the average number the payroll would be $260,000. If you add some additional salary for managers and high quality technicians, then the number could be $300,000.

The income statement reflected salaries and wages of $250,000 the first year and $100,000 the second year. Of this amount, $40,000 each year was allocated to owner's salary. The owner declared that he didn't work there. The obvious inaccuracy in reporting the wages and salaries is another red flag.

It is possible that all of these concerns and seeming irregularities could be explained to the satisfaction of a buyer. However, if the interest is substantial on the part of the buyer, an audit of the financials and a complete inventory, including the identification of obsolete inventory, would be in order, as well as a review of payroll reports and sales tax reports to the state.

The numbers need to add up, especially with inexplicable red flags.

Whether you are selling a business or buying a business, you should be aware of the importance of the buyer's need to have a reliable understanding of the company, whether investigated entirely by the buyer or by experienced professionals who know what red flags to be aware of and to watch for in the financial review.

A Case for Liquidation

PRECISION GRINDING COMPANY P&L Comparisons 2001 - 2002		
	2001	2002
Sales	529,700	433,356
Cost of Goods Sold	299,415	240,733
Gross Profit	**230,285**	**192,623**

The above section indicates a healthy profit margin but very limited gross revenue for a manufacturing company. A manufacturing company such as this is typically capital intensive due to equipment costs, which must be considered in changing technologies and maintenance issues.

The sales reflects a decline of almost 20% over the previous year.

Expenses		
Auto	7,960	11,639
Depreciation	1,699	1,479
Dues & Subscriptions	287	504
Equipment Rental	42,788	36,000
Insurance - General	6,085	10,546
Insurance - Health	25,755	28,622
Interest	3,168	
Laundry	3,169	1,846
Legal & Professional	10,929	4,970
Office Expense		1,926
Payroll Services	2,182	
Pension Plan Costs	4,702	5,716
Postage	309	692
Promotion	2,941	2,513
Rent	39,000	33,000
Repairs & Maintenance	10,402	9,411
Salaries - Officers	20,000	
Salaries & Wages	33,344	27,327
Taxes & Licenses	27,816	15,390
Telephone	4,006	4,660
Travel	408	438
Utilities	17,288	17,853
Total Expenses	**264,240**	**214,532**
Other Income	1,148	330
Net Income Before Taxes	**32,807)**	**(21,579)**

OPERATING FINANCIAL MODELS

The owner's income primarily was received from rent for the premises which he owned personally and rent for some of the equipment which he owned personally. The above section indicates that the owner was not well-paid in salary and, in year two, he received less rent for the premises, less rent for equipment and no salary. After all operating expenses were deducted there was no net income in either year. There simply was insufficient revenue to cover basic operating expenses.

Adjustments			
Owner Compensation		20,000	
Owner Payroll Taxes		1,600	
Depreciation		1,699	1,479
Interest		3,168	
Interest & Dividends		(1,148)	(330)
Eqpt Rent paid to Owner		41,788	36,000
Total Adjustments		67,107	37,149
Discretionary Earnings		**34,300**	**15,570**

This owner was seeking an exit plan for retirement. After the value considerations which were derived from the future potential earnings, the decision was made to liquidate the operating assets by selling the equipment on the open market to competitors or by auction, and to lease the building to another business to provide ongoing income for the owner.

Conclusion

MAKING THE DECISION to become self-employed requires some soul-searching. The decision to forgo a regular paycheck can be a stressful process. It can mean walking away from the confidence of others that you have earned during your employment. It can mean abandoning opportunities to continue up the promotion chain of management in larger companies. It can mean losing the position and pride of individual value in a smaller company. It can mean taking the risk of declining income for an extended period of time. If your entry into the world of the entrepreneur is less than adequately successful, it can mean a costly delay in building your status and income as an employee of a company with sustainability and growth prospects.

For the individual with ambition, self-assurance, good work ethic, self-motivation, and reasonable tolerance for the pressure of management responsibility, owning a business or another method of self-employment can be very rewarding. It can be rewarding through the satisfaction and pride of success, the feeling of independence, financial reward, accumulating future retirement value in your own enterprise - or all of the above.

It can also be disappointing if things don't turn out as planned. The ability to tolerate adversity could be considered a prerequisite for business ownership. Many entrepreneurs have had initial failures but have gone on to be very successful in other enterprises. Some fail and decide that employment with others is a better career path to maximize the reward from their employment experience. So, in either case, a fallback position can be of value.

CONCLUSION

There are millions of successful business ventures in this country. They all started out small with the ideas and hopes of one or more individuals. Many of them grew to be viable small or mid-sized businesses. Many of them grew to become big companies. And a select number grew to become behemoth corporations on an international scale. The simplest businesses and the most complex businesses took many of the same requirements: an idea, a business plan, financial planning, financial resources, work ethic, a positive attitude, diligence, tenacity, understanding, capacity for change, promotion, hard work, and the willingness to stay the course.

As was mentioned in the introduction to this book, if you would like to be your own boss, have more control over your future income and success, run a business the way you think best, make your own decisions, hire whom you like, serve whom you like, set your own hours, reap the rewards from your efforts, build value in the business that you can redeem personally at some point, either in a future sale of the enterprise or through absentee management in retirement, or maybe work at the rest of your life at whatever level you desire – owning your own business could be the answer for you.

To give your endeavor the best chance of success you should understand the line of business you choose to pursue. You should know it inside and out. You should know what will make it succeed and what can lead to failure. You should prepare your business plan around the facets of the business that ensure success and guard against those which could cause failure. You should assure yourself and prepare yourself to assure others of your understanding of the challenges. You should make sure you are capitalized initially to the level required, with reserves for the unexpected. Choose the location carefully, select any staffing requirements carefully, and identify the risk factors carefully. You should discuss your plans with trusted advisors to identify factors that you may have overlooked.

At the same time, you should be aware that there is always an element of risk no matter how careful the planning. However, don't overthink the risk factors to the point of discouragement. You shouldn't expect to find an error-proof or failure-proof business venture. The important thing in managing risk is to assure yourself that the accepted risks won't sink the ship, that you can survive by making changes or survive by changing direction or abandoning ship and launching a new venture. Forget that old advice about the captain going down with the ship. That doesn't apply in the business world.

When all else fails, seek advice. Seeking advice is not a sign of failure or incompetence; it is a good management practice. We all need advice sometimes. The largest corporations in the world have a board of directors to give advice when needed. Choose your advisors carefully. Every company that was ever founded made mistakes. If you can bat safely in baseball one time out of four, you are a superstar. You can't expect to bat perfectly in your own business. You just need to exercise your management ability and your prudence to manage your risks effectively.

Remaining financially healthy is imperative for growing a business. Burdensome debt obligations can impair growth. Bank loans and easy credit sounds great, but it all has to be repaid and has to be serviced constantly in the process of building and operating your business. Very few businesses grow without debt. However, very few businesses without debt fail. It is most often debt that sinks a business in challenging times. Just as a ship without ballast would be more likely to sink in a storm, a business that is top-heavy with debt and weak in foundation can be difficult to keep afloat.

Of course, adequate capital is a must in growing any business. Very few of the largest companies in the world can generate income fast enough to fund their expansion. That is why the stock market came about over a hundred years ago, to provide capital for corporate expansion or the founding of new enterprises. The larger companies sell shares of stock in the company or use bond issues to acquire growth capital. Unfortunately, the alternative of selling shares of stock or issuing bonds in a small enterprise is rarely available.

Sometimes a general partnership or limited partnership is a viable alternative. In such an arrangement, the principal who started

CONCLUSION

the enterprise gives up portions of ownership in order to generate capital to move forward with the expansion plans without the burden of debt service that could sink the ship. This is a path that more small business owners should entertain. It removes the stress of debt repayment and often creates an ongoing source of funding for companies with good growth potential. The ownership of a portion of a successful enterprise is much favored over full ownership of a company burdened with debt and stymied from pursuing growth opportunities. Someone once said: ten percent of something is better than a hundred percent of nothing. I guess that would depend on what ten percent of something amounts to. This is not to advise you to settle for ten percent ownership of your enterprise, especially if you are doing all the work. Any combination of business ownership must make sense for all concerned. Any combination of business ownership should have a plan to provide commensurate remuneration for risk as well as effort. It should include a plan for dissolution of ownership, parting due to irreconcilable differences, and a plan for bringing on new ownership if needed for capital or management purposes. All of these ownership scenarios are not prerequisite choices but can be altered as needed for expansion or financial stability. The important element is an open mind and willingness to make the prudent decision regarding the best alternatives for you and your enterprise, for growth, for survival, for peace of mind, and for building a company of whatever size that makes self-employment work for you.

A significant amount of detail was offered in this guide about franchises. The reason is that a franchise would be a recommended entry into the business ownership world for many who seek self-employment but lack a clear direction into business ownership or lack self-confidence in achieving success in the launch of a new enterprise or assumption of a going concern. With a carefully selected franchise, those with a lack of experience in a particular type of business, limited funding for an acquisition or start-up, or lack of general business management experience, would often have a better chance of success by taking advantage of a proven business plan which has been established over time by a successful franchisor. This may be a good alternative, at least for a period of learning general business practices for some who have limited direction toward a given industry and limited business knowledge. The risk of failure is generally much less for franchisees of well-established franchise operations. Also, many franchisors enable ownership of multiple franchises for those who choose to increase their income.

The key to success in your chosen path to self-employment could be stated in the cliché of a mentor of mine many years ago: *"plan your work and work your plan."* That is a simple yet a profound way of stating what we have just discussed throughout this self-employment, business ownership guide.

In planning your work and working your plan you should consider the essential steps in the process of engaging in business ownership:

Know yourself: 1) carefully select the business or industry to pursue, 2) understand the management expertise required, 3) identify the market for your product or service, 4) calculate the financial requirements, 5) establish a financial plan for acquisition or start-up, 6) establish a plan for the operation of the enterprise, 7) and understand the potential risks or causes of failure.

Recognize the fact that it is easy to get over-enthusiastic about the value or potential of a business enterprise, either in a start-up or the acquisition of a going business. Even in the financially astute world of the private equity groups, over-enthusism or unreasonable expectations can cause overpayment or disappointing investment results. So the importance of caution and planning cannot be overestimated in any size transaction.

All of this is called planning your work. Once that is accomplished satisfactorily, you can work your plan and have more control over your future livelihood and success.

CONCLUSION

You will be better prepared to:

- Start a business
- Make it a success
- Keep the profits
- Build your future
- Be your own boss

In a Business of Your Own!

Glossary of Financial Terms Used in this Publication

Accounts Receivable – amounts owed to company by customers for goods sold or services rendered

Accounts Payable – amounts owed to suppliers by company for goods or services purchased

Acquisition – purchasing or buying - acquiring a business

Amortization – deduction as an expense of a portion of the cost of certain intangible costs over a specified period of time, such as: organizational expenses, patents, copyrights

Asset – any tangible item owned by a company, such as furniture, fixtures, equipment. Also, any intangible item owned by the company, such as patents and copyrights

Balance Sheet – a financial statement which lists all assets at cost, all liabilities at the balance owed and the capital structure, including invested capital, stock sales and retained earnings

Cash Flow – net income of the business, plus non-cash expenses, such as depreciation and amortization

Cost of Goods Sold – purchased material, direct labor and other items directly required to provide goods or services sold

Depreciation – deduction as an expense of a portion of the cost of assets of the company as the asset loses value

Discretionary Earnings – earnings of the company, plus owner benefits, perquisites and non-business related expenses, paid by the company

Divestitures – the sale or other disposition of a company or portion thereof

Earnings – profits of the company as expressed in various forms, such as earnings before taxes, earnings after taxes, earnings before taxes, depreciation and amortization, discretionary earnings

EAT– Earnings after taxes

EBIT – Earnings before interest and taxes

EBITDA – Earnings before interest, taxes, depreciation and amortization

EBITDA+OC – EBITDA plus owner's compensation

Entrepreneur – One who organizes and manages a business enterprise

Entrepreneurship - the act of organizing and managing a business enterprise

Franchise – an agreement or license to utilize procedures, a brand name, or to buy or sell a product or service, granted to another by an established company or individual

Franchisee – a party granted a franchise agreement

Franchisor – a party granting a franchise agreement

Goodwill – a value placed on the reputation of the company, owner relationships and operational techniques that enhance the value of the company. A portion of the sale price not considered tangible assets

Gross Profit – total sales of the business less the direct costs of goods sold, not including operating expenses

Intangible Assets – assets other than furniture, fixtures and equipment, such as: patents, copyrights, goodwill, trade secrets, franchises, distribution rights

Inventory – all goods provided for sale by a company either as raw material, work in process or finished goods

Mergers – joining two or more companies to operate as one

Operating Expenses – general and administrative expenses not directly allocated to merchandise or services sold to customers, such as rent, office expenses, insurance, payroll, telephone, utilities, etc.

Net Profit – profit of the company after deducting cost of goods and operating expenses

PEG – Private equity group, an investment group that acquires businesses

Perquisites – benefits received by the owner other than monetary remuneration

Risk Premium – an adjustment to value based on the risk of loss of, a return on or a return of the investment or any portion thereof

Tangible Assets – furniture, fixtures, equipment, tools – sometimes referred to as fixed assets,

Working Capital – capital required to finance normal operations, such as cash on hand and accounts receivable

Index

A
Accounting 16, 19
Accounting irregularities 140
Acquisition criteria 43
Acquisition valuation 41
Assets 9

B
Bank loans 80, 82
Business characteristics 34
Business expansion 113
Business plan 49, 67
Business plan format 53
Business plan illustration 55, 71
Business operations 9
Business organizations 7
Business statistics 3
Business types 23
Buying a business 38

C
Conclusion 144
Corporation 8
Cost of sales 11, 151

D
Documentation 47
Due diligence 46
Duties of entrepreneurs 5

E
EAT 152
EBIT 152
EBITDA 152
EBITDA+OC 152
Entrepreneur 5, 152
Entrepreneurship 1, 152

F
Financial models 130
Financing 80, 89
Franchises 87, 92
Franchise history 91
Franchise opportunities 101, 110
Franchise ratings 103, 104

G
General partnership 7
Glossary of terms 151
Gross profit 11, 153

H
Historical earnings 40

I
Insurance 12
Integration 47

L
Laws, rules, regulations 15
Liabilities 9
Limited liability company 8
Limited partnership 7
Liquidation, a case 142

M
Marketing implementation 114
Marketing methods 115
Mergers & Acquisitions 117, 153

N
Negotiating agreement 45

O
Objectives of buyer 39, 73
Operating expenses 11

P
Payroll records 13
PEG criteria 123
PEG priorities 123
PEGs 122
Private equity groups 122
Profit margin 11
Public company 8
Purchase agreement terms 45

R
Red flags 140
Revenue 9
Risks to consider 44

S

Subchapter S – Corp. 8
Sanity test 42, 137, 138
SBA 4, 83, 119
Self-employment 17
Seller financing 81
Small Business Admin. 4, 83, 119
Sole practitioner 18
Sole proprietorship 7
Starting a business 63

T

Taxation considerations 46
Transition assistance 47
Type of business 23

U

Under capitalization 67
Unreasonable expectations 68

V

Valuation considerations 41
Value drivers 43

W

Working capital 64

www.ingramcontent.com/pod-product-compliance
Lightning Source LLC
Chambersburg PA
CBHW031054180526
45163CB00002BA/835